Cambridge Elements

Elements in Philosophy of Law

SUBSIDIARITY

Andreas Follesdal
University of Oslo

Shaftesbury Road, Cambridge CB2 8EA, United Kingdom

One Liberty Plaza, 20th Floor, New York, NY 10006, USA

477 Williamstown Road, Port Melbourne, VIC 3207, Australia

314–321, 3rd Floor, Plot 3, Splendor Forum, Jasola District Centre, New Delhi – 110025, India

103 Penang Road, #05–06/07, Visioncrest Commercial, Singapore 238467

Cambridge University Press is part of Cambridge University Press & Assessment, a department of the University of Cambridge.

We share the University's mission to contribute to society through the pursuit of education, learning and research at the highest international levels of excellence.

www.cambridge.org
Information on this title: www.cambridge.org/9781009571654

DOI: 10.1017/9781108993685

When citing this work, please include a reference to the DOI 10.1017/9781108993685

First published 2025

A catalogue record for this publication is available from the British Library

ISBN 978-1-009-57165-4 Hardback
ISBN 978-1-108-99523-8 Paperback
ISSN 2631-5815 (online)
ISSN 2631-5807 (print)

Subsidiarity

Elements in Philosophy of Law

DOI: 10.1017/9781108993685
First published online: February 2025

Andreas Follesdal
University of Oslo

Author for correspondence: Andreas Follesdal, andreas@follesdal.net

Abstract: 'Subsidiarity' is vague and contested, yet popular in scholarship about international law due to its role in the European Union (EU). Which conceptions of subsidiarity are more justifiable, and how might they contribute to international law? A principle of subsidiarity concerns how to establish, allocate, or use authority within a social or legal order, stating a rebuttable presumption for the local. Various historical patterns, practices, principles, and justifications offer different recommendations. Seven normative theories vary in how immunity-protecting or person-promoting they are. The latter appear more justifiable and withstand criticism often raised against subsidiarity. Some conceptions of person-promoting subsidiarity serve as a structuring principle for international law and fulfil several criteria of a general principle of law. It can harmonize domestic and international law but is not sufficient to reduce fragmentation among sectors with different objectives. This title is also available as Open Access on Cambridge Core.

Keywords: subsidiarity, international law, European Union, European Court of Human Rights, general principle of law

ISBNs: 9781009571654 (HB), 9781108995238 (PB), 9781108993685 (OC)
ISSNs: 2631-5815 (online), 2631-5807 (print)

Contents

1 Introduction 1

PART I HISTORICAL AND SYSTEMATIC ACCOUNTS OF SUBSIDIARITY 5

2 Traditions of Subsidiarity: Patterns, Practices, Principles 5

3 Elements of Subsidiarity 14

4 Theories of Subsidiarity 17

5 Modest Conclusions 35

PART II SUBSIDIARITY IN INTERNATIONAL LAW 36

6 Subsidiarity: A General Principle of Law? 36

7 Inter-systemic Coherence: Human Rights and State Sovereignty 43

8 Inter-systemic Coherence: Subsidiarity in the European Union 48

9 Intra-systemic Coherence and Subsidiarity: Human Rights in Europe 54

10 Conclusions 60

References 66

Acknowledgements 92

1 Introduction

A principle of subsidiarity concerns how to *establish*, *allocate*, or *use* authority. It states a *rebuttable presumption for the more local unit* – a presumption for more proximate authority. Or so this Element maintains.

'Subsidiarity' has become a popular term in scholarship about international law, not least due to its role in the European Union (EU). Several authors also nominate subsidiarity as a 'structuring principle' for international law, or even for global or planetary governance (Lamy 2012 in Broude 2016: 57). Yet the term 'subsidiarity' is so vague and contested that an essay on it may seem Sisyphean (Van Kersbergen and Verbeek 2007). It is perhaps among the concepts that 'make perfect sense in practice but for which it seems impossible to develop a theory' (Howse and Nicolaïdis 2016: 259). Clarity may even threaten its usefulness: allegedly 'subsidiarity' quelled fears of centralized authority to the EU and the European Court of Human Rights (ECtHR) only due to obfuscation (Lecheler 1993, Marquardt 1994, Fabbrini 2018).

Yet it is premature to conclude that 'subsidiarity' is an essentially contested concept 'which inevitably involves endless disputes about their proper uses' (Gallie 1956: 169). Any such conclusion is provisional. Few have addressed and assessed its philosophical underpinnings, especially outside the EU context. Systematic reflection may at least raise 'the level of quality of arguments in the disputes' (193), reduce obscurity, and strengthen criticisms. Or so this volume seeks to show. Attention to features and justifications of different conceptions of subsidiarity helps us understand where we disagree, what is at stake, what are better accounts, and how and when – if at all – subsidiarity might be of service, in international law and elsewhere.

Critics object that it offers Eurocentric support for unjust institutions ranging from the patriarchal family to colonial empire. Subsidiarity is said to offer only instrumentalist excuses for existing institutions, ignoring any intrinsic value they may have, yet offers no critical standards to assess them. In international law subsidiarity protects sovereign states unduly against interference and obligations, even wicked regimes (Dyzenhaus 2010), and even against collective responses avert human rights tragedies or climate crises. The present reflections do not defend any theory of subsidiarity against these charges. Reflection may identify, strengthen, and assess criticisms of subsidiarity, and perhaps improve our responses.

This Element assumes that a principle of subsidiarity concerns how to *establish*, *allocate*, or *use* authority within a social, political, or legal order, including reviewing the actions of other bodies. Subsidiarity states a rebuttable presumption for the local (Kaufmann 1988, Blichner and Sangolt 1994, Follesdal 1998). It places the burden of argument with attempts to centralize authority: Tasks or legal powers should rest with the more local unit unless allocating them to a more central unit achieves certain objectives more efficiently or effectively.

Compare subsidiarity principles to some alternatives. We may need no ordering principle among authorities (Bull 1977: 264–769) – witness the plethora of treaties states have used to solve their problems. A *list* may allocate authority over specific issues, as in the EU. A third alternative could be a (rebuttable) preference for *centralized* authority, for instance, as when a constitution leaves unmentioned authority with central authorities. Yet another alternative is the 'all-affected' principle, that those affected by decisions should decide (Dahl 1970: 49, Whelan 1983, Goodin 2007). Some have used 'subsidiarity' in this sense (Held 2004: 374, Barber 2018: 187).

1.1 Overview

Part 1 of these reflections starts with the many versions of subsidiarity and turns to assess which of them may be more normatively justifiable. Part 2 considers how subsidiarity may contribute to justify international law and operate within it. Space limitations require that references to others' contributions replace detailed arguments. Any contributions are philosophical rather than legal. The reflections might at best guide international legal scholars faced with the highly 'ambiguous or obscure' term 'subsidiarity' in treaties, or who ask whether subsidiarity is, or should be, a source of international law in the form of a 'general principle of law'.

The definition of subsidiarity deliberately leaves many issues open, which different *conceptions* of subsidiarity specify differently. *Theories* of subsidiarity offer normative justifications of some of these conceptions: why and when actors might regard a particular conception of subsidiarity as a binding rule so that use of authority consistent with that conception is more legitimate.

Section 2 provides examples, expressions, and justifications of subsidiarity in several cultures and continents. These traditions exhibit *patterns* of behaviour, rules of social or legal *practices*, and use subsidiarity as legal *principles* for institutional design and review. Our main interest is not the patterns of behaviour we may describe in terms of subsidiarity, but rather practices where actors are guided by reference to subsidiarity or similar presumptions (Manning 2011, Waldron 2013). The sketches are not authoritative accounts but rather invitations to 'deparochialize' this topic (Williams 2020). They still challenge views that subsidiarity is only a European tradition serving to protect state immunity.

Section 3 provides a taxonomy of elements that vary among conceptions of subsidiarity: which institutions to have, how to allocate authority among them, and how they should use it. The theories differ about the objectives of the polity, the domains and roles of local units and central bodies, and who they grant the authority to decide such issues. The variations have striking institutional implications.

Section 4 summarizes six normative justifications for various such conceptions, from Immunity, Non-domination, Freedom, Efficiency, Perfectionist Justice, and Legitimacy. All justify authority by how it protects or furthers various interests of individual persons who are regarded as the ultimate unit of normative concern. The order of presentation roughly reflects the decreasing immunity of local units and increased attention to relations 'below' the state down to persons. The former, more *immunity-preserving* conceptions are less convincing than the later, *person-promoting* conceptions of subsidiarity. Many of the former are European, while the latter more justifiable versions include some also found outside Europe.

Section 5 draws six observations that help respond to the objections mentioned earlier, and which have implications for international law. The different accounts yield widely different conclusions about who should have what sorts of authority. They only contribute more specific conclusions when the ultimate objectives are given. Some theories support distributive obligations across local units, for instance, due to unfair starting points or unfair division of benefits from cooperation. Other accounts perpetuate injustice as we may see it. The more immunity-preserving theories only consider the risk to individuals of domination or tyranny by external bodies, they ignore issues of distributive justice among local units, and they lack 'quality control' concerning how local authorities treat individuals within or outside their borders. The 'person-promoting' conceptions of subsidiarity are less objectionable, but also offer weaker support for subsidiarity.

Part 2 considers contributions of subsidiarity about and within international law.

One central concern is that international law seems to fit better with the less justifiable immunity-preserving conceptions of subsidiarity than with person-promoting conceptions. This may challenge the normative legitimacy of international law. However, person-promoting conceptions may also explain, structure, and perhaps justify many aspects of international law. A second topic is to explore possible contributions of such conceptions of subsidiarity to international law. To present and assess these we consider whether subsidiarity may share the characteristics and provide the services of 'general principles of law' – one source of international law. The aim is only philosophical, to clarify and assess some possible roles of subsidiarity. Legal arguments that subsidiarity is, or should be, such a source of international law are beyond the objectives of this Element.

Section 6 addresses claims that subsidiarity serves, or should serve, as a 'structuring principle' to render international law more ordered and coherent in ways we have reason to value. Some person-promoting conceptions of subsidiarity explain some state-centric *patterns* of international law. They may also serve as a *principle* for attempts to harmonize it, and as a *rule* in the international legal practices of legislators and courts. Person-promoting conceptions of subsidiarity also satisfy several conditions for being a 'general principle' of international law. Subsidiarity may bring cohesion to the international legal system and more coherence between it and domestic legal systems. Some subsidiarity conceptions occur in many national legal systems and are also formed within the international legal system, thus satisfying the pedigree of general principles. Person-promoting conceptions can be transposed to the international legal system and are compatible with its immunity-protecting features, appearances notwithstanding. Of course, these modest conclusions do not suffice to determine whether subsidiarity is, or should be, such a general principle of law.

Sections 7 and 8 explore how subsidiarity may contribute to 'inter-systemic' coherence between international and domestic legal orders. The cases show how more immunity-protecting and more person-promoting conceptions alleviate tensions in drastically different ways.

The immunity-protecting conceptions of subsidiarity fit well with what some scholars now identify as Authoritarian International Law (Ginsburg 2020: 224). Some states use international law to reinforce their own sovereign immunity. They even hollow out the accountability mechanisms of international or regional human rights treaties with independent monitoring bodies. In contrast the person-promoting conceptions of subsidiarity support international expressions of concern through international law, and more independent human rights bodies that hold state powers accountable.

Both versions of subsidiarity require regional human rights institutions to defer to states – but in strikingly divergent ways. We consider the Human Rights Declaration of the Association of Southeast Asian Nations (ASEAN) and the ECtHR with its 'margin of appreciation' doctrine. Considerations of subsidiarity alone do not guide the choice among these alternatives that give strikingly different priority to human rights or sovereignty.

Section 8 explores subsidiarity in the EU, its history and current practice to foster inter-systemic coherence. The conception may be person-promoting, even though it might appear otherwise, due to the human rights constraints on membership in the EU.

Section 9 explores a limit to the usefulness of subsidiarity. It may foster limited 'intra-systemic' coherence among different sectors of international law but cannot on its own resolve the choice among alternative modes of coherence. One reason is that different treaties have divergent objectives. Subsidiarity in two European legal orders that both protect human rights illustrates this: the EU treaties and its Court of Justice of the EU (CJEU), versus the European Convention on Human Rights (ECHR) and its ECtHR. Subsidiarity arguments may justify both, but do not resolve tensions between these legal orders when they grant primacy of market freedoms *or* of human rights, respectively. So subsidiarity helps only when ultimate objectives are given.

Section 10 draws some modest conclusions. It responds to the objections raised against subsidiarity and then considers how subsidiarity may contribute to international law. More justifiable theories of subsidiarity are not immunity-protecting, so they challenge the current strong presumptions of state immunity and veto. Person-promoting subsidiarity may instead support attempts to give individuals more prominence. Some person-promoting conceptions of subsidiarity may also satisfy several characteristics of general principles of law regarding their sources, and they may contribute some convergence and coherence to international law. However, a principle of subsidiarity alone cannot serve as a 'meta-authority' to resolve intra-systemic conflicts among authorities (Zürn 2018: 37). That would require an authoritative specification and ordering of the objectives of the political or legal order.

PART I HISTORICAL AND SYSTEMATIC ACCOUNTS OF SUBSIDIARITY

2 Traditions of Subsidiarity: Patterns, Practices, Principles

To understand how conceptions of subsidiarity vary we can look for *patterns* of behaviour, parts of *practices*, or more or less explicit *principles* for institutional design and for the exercise of authority across time and space. We find subsidiarity on several continents, in a broad range of religions and philosophies. The examples show that subsidiarity is not only a Western or Eurocentric phenomenon. They all appear to regard human persons and their interests as the ultimate unit of moral concern. Many of them question the state as central and immune from intervention.

Note that when subsidiarity simply describes a pattern of political or legal order the participants need not be aware of any such rules. And even if they are aware of a rule they might not see a reason to comply with it. Some such 'habits' may be relevant for whether subsidiarity is an 'international custom' or a 'general practice accepted as law' (Statute of the International Court of Justice (ICJ) 1946: Art. 38(1). So for our purposes the important cases are *practices*: when a conception of subsidiarity (if not by that name) appears to claim authority that participants regard as binding when they deliberate about creating, modifying, reviewing, or assessing a practice (Hart 1994, Shapiro 2006, Raz 2017: 140). It is subsidiarity as part of such practices rather than mere descriptions of a pattern that are most relevant for its possible contribution to international law.

2.1 Patterns

We might describe several patterns of social organization in many communities by the term 'subsidiarity', even some that predate written sources. Several practices also have stated rules which express what we may recognize as subsidiarity, often specifying both who has primary responsibility and who may or should act in case those primarily responsible fail. The practices give different actors de facto authority to make decisions. Such patterns appear to concern the *use* of authority only, not as a guide to institutional design. One limitation of some of the patterns is that they only concern two levels of bodies beyond the individual, rather than exhibiting a more general rule to give preference for the more local unit.

The tribal organization of the Māori in what is now New Zealand included family groups (*whanau*) who would work together and collaborate for defence as a clan (*hapū*). The tribe (*iwi)* would in turn operate as a federation among several *hapū* for common defence (Ballara 1998: 19, Gussen 2014).

Several extinct African societies had structures we may describe by subsidiarity. The legal order of Igboland – now in Nigeria – had a preference for more local bodies (Ike and Edozien 2001: Ch. 6, 8). Elements of social and political ordering of the Tiv people in Nigeria also illustrate subsidiarity (Iber 2011: 21), as do the loose confederation of Hausa city-states (Yoo 2009), and the checks and balances of the Yoruba monarchical structure (Lloyd 1971, Usman and Falola 2019). We can use subsidiarity to describe features of pre-fourteenth-century Ganda society, in what later became the kingdom of the Baganda, now part of Uganda. The power structures between the chief (*ssabataka*) and heads of tribes *(mutaka*) were one of primus inter pares. The legitimate tasks of the central unit were limited to promoting the well-being of the lower units, 'aiding them to realize their good and their potential' (Wamala 2004: 436–437). The tribes enjoyed immunity in the sense that the central units should not usurp the responsibilities of the lower units of power. A dissatisfied *mutaka* could even withdraw from the jurisdiction of the *ssabataka* – that is, exercise a right to exit. Then, as now, the possibility of exit gives local units more de facto power to ensure that a central ruler serves their interests. The local units might thus specify and apply what we can describe as arguments of subsidiarity about what should be done by whom.

Nahua (Aztek) culture illustrates multi-level subsidiarity. *Tlaxilacalli* – 'neighbourhoods' – usually submitted to the authority of the sovereign local polity, or *altepetl*, which then scaled up to autonomous mega-provinces (*huei altepetl*) and finally to the entire empire. At each level, submission was traded for autonomy, undercutting any attempt at direct centralizing rule (Johnson 2017: 4, cf. Espejo 2012: 1061). We see a pattern of subsidiarity in the 1428 triple alliance for military purposes among the three city-states (*altepetl*) of Tenochtitlan, Texcoco, and Totoquihuatzin. Each of these ruled over their dependent *altepetl* without interference by the other two (Lockhart 1992, Berdan 2017).

2.2 Confucian Familial Subsidiarity

The Confucian political philosopher Mencius (379–298 BC) laid out a three-step allocation of responsibility for the well-being of the individual (Chan 2003). The roles and responsibilities among members of the family over generations are central components of the freedom of every individual (Sun 2020: 49). In this 'familial' model the family has primary responsibility for those unable to care for themselves, and rulers are regarded as the *parents* of the people (Mencius 2003: 1B.13). Note the commitment to individuals: 'The people are the most crucial and important [element of society], next is the state, least is the king' (Bojun 1980: 328, from Zhao 2015). When the family *could not* assist, the community network *should* provide support. Only when the community was *unable* would what we now may describe as the more centralized body have *an obligation* to aid.

Mencius' conception of subsidiarity constrains central action. Rulers' taxes must not render people unable to perform their duties (Duke Wen of Teng 1: 155). The units' immunity is supplemented by the rulers' *positive* obligation to empower them: Those who cannot sustain themselves should be given help to do so (IB.4). Some of the centre's supportive obligations are listed and justified: In agricultural communities the ruler of the state is responsible for 'Old men without wives, old women without husbands, old people without children, young children without fathers – these four types of people are *the most destitute and have no one to turn to for help*' (IB.5, emphasis added). The *Book of Rites* adds the disabled and the sick to this list (Confucius 200 BC (1885)).

The ruler must also maintain granaries as a last resort for these groups, at pains of regicide (Mencius: King Hui of Liang, part Two, p. 55). The Song dynasty (960–1279) and the Ming dynasty (1368–1644) had such granaries, and officials were punished if they failed these obligations (Huan-Chang 1911, Chan 2012: 88–89). But in general the rulers did not heed Confucius' and Mencius' views (Zhao 2015, 190).

Some argue that aspects of this Confucian tradition still inform the social welfare regimes of some East Asian countries, at least to the extent that the authorities choose to appeal to this heritage to justify their 'residualist' model of low levels of public social protection (Goodman and Peng 1996, Walker and Wong 2005, Kongshøj 2015). This tradition of strong immunity of the lower units may also be one of several factors that explain the relatively weak regional institutions in Asia (cf. Section 7.1).

2.3 Aristotelian Subsidiarity

Aristotle's (384–322 BC) account of the functions of political units illustrates practices of subsidiarity. The tasks of households and villages are to secure individuals' necessities of life. The city-state (*polis*) is a community of such households, clans, and villages, for their protection and fulfilment (Politics: III.9, 1280b).

Observe that the interests of individuals are the ultimate focus of moral and political concern, and that these include the intrinsic value for individuals of the broader society. Aristotle underscores that membership in a *polis* is not only instrumental to human beings, but a component of a full human life. Humanity (*anthropos*) is by nature a 'political animal' (*politikon zoon*). The good life and purpose of humans can only be fully secured and fulfilled in the self-sufficient *polis* (Politics: I.2, 1252b, 1253, 1278b19-20). Some of Aristotle's arguments in defence of the status quo of Greek society have had long-lasting repercussions, some deplorable – such that 'women, slaves, and artisans and traders are all subsidiary instruments for the achievements of the highest happiness of "man"' (Okin 1979 (2013)): ch 4, Smith 1983). This flaw underscores the importance of *who* has the authority to identify both the institutions and the objectives to which subsidiarity applies.

2.4 Subsidiarity in Islam – *Zakat*

Islamic thought expresses subsidiarity as a practice and as a pillar of Islam, concerning *zakat* – obligatory charity or 'alm tax' (Blecher 2020) provided to certain needy persons. The Arabic term 'zakat' means purity, but can also mean justness, integrity, honesty, righteousness, or goodness (Zysow 2012, Wehr and Cowan 2020). These meanings also indicate several of its justifications. *Zakat* secures a more just economic distribution and hence purifies one's own wealth; it expresses the dignity, also of the poor, and aims to secure their independence; and fosters virtue rather than greed among the givers (Qur'an 9: 103, Bonner 2005). *Zakat* supplements the obligations family members have towards each other, to reduce the risk that anyone must beg others for sustenance. Indeed, a husband may not count such support to his household as his *zakat*. In addition, every able Muslim must provide a proportion of their net wealth – 2.5–20 per cent – to support others in need. Different Islamic law states and different Islamic legal traditions specify the relevant wealth differently.

The categories of need and the form of support are specified and limited, reminiscent of the aforementioned Confucian list:

> The alms are only for the poor and the needy, and those who collect them, and those whose hearts are to be reconciled, and to free the captives and the debtors, and for the cause of Allah, and (for) the wayfarers . . . (Qur'an 9:60, for more elaborate lists cf. Zysow 2012)

The Prophet Mohammad urged individuals to support in accordance with what we may describe as a positive and empowering conception of subsidiarity. According to Abū Da'wūd's collection of prophetic sayings and practices, the Prophet helped a beggar become financially self-sufficient, rather than simply giving him money. The latter would only be appropriate for those *unable* to work (Zysow 2012)

We may regard this as a pattern or even a principle of subsidiarity concerning the *allocation* and *use* of authority: Support those who cannot support themselves and whose next of kin cannot do so, preferably in ways that facilitate their self reliance.

Concerning the allocation of authority, note the contested role of the state when it comes to assess, collect, and distribute *zakat*. *Zakat* may have limited the state's arbitrary power to tax and reduced the risk of corruption (Blecher 2020). The practices illustrate alternative conceptions of subsidiarity regarding whether private or public bodies have primary responsibilities to assess, collect, and distribute the *zakat* (Qur'an 9: 103). In some states the collection or distribution of *zakat*, sometimes tax deductible, is the responsibility of quasi-governmental or civil society organizations or mosques (Zysow 2012). In other states it is the government's responsibility either to manage the whole system or to ensure that *zakat* is managed if Muslims fail to pay.

2.5 An *Ubuntu* Conception of Subsidiarity

The African philosophy of *Ubuntu* applies a conception of subsidiarity that has survived and developed both as a philosophical position and as a legal theory.

The term 'Ubuntu' stems from the Nguni phrase *Umuntu ngumuntu ngabantu*: 'A person is a person through other persons.' *Ubuntu* emphasizes the harmonious relationships between persons as constitutive of the individual and underscores compassion and commitment to one another's growth: 'I am, because we are; and since we are, therefore, I am' (Mbiti 1969: 141), 'One becomes a moral person insofar as one honours communal relationships' (Eze 2008: 106, Metz 2011: 540, Metz 2021).

The term has been used in strikingly different ways, from a concept of sin to an expression of emancipation, so we should be cognizant of the risks of undue imposition and simplification (Stråth 2023: 56–93). Such cautions notwithstanding, note that Shutte develops an *Ubuntu* version of subsidiarity in support of self-determination of humans and their communities. The task of governments at various levels is to promote harmonious flourishing and community – *ubuntu* – of the constituent parts when needed (Shutte 2001: 379–381). This is yet another example of how the commitment to the individual's good as having fundamental moral worth includes as a constitutive part acting for the sake of others, and without allowing total sacrifice of an individual for the collective (Metz 2007).

While *Ubuntu* is often criticized as too vague, recent contributions lay some such concerns to rest (Ramose 1999, Shutte 2001, Metz 2007, 2011). Gädeke discerns Perfectionist and Relational conceptions of *Ubuntu*. The latter is similar to neo-republican theories in political philosophy and recognizes relationships of sharing and caring (Gädeke 2009: 282–283). How to apply this conception of subsidiarity is contested, for instance, concerning the care and support women should get from their fathers or husbands (Cornell 2012: 329).

Ubuntu was included in the epilogue of the 1993 Interim Constitution of South Africa, but not explicitly in its 1996 Constitution. We arguably see expressions of the *Ubuntu* tradition – and subsidiarity – in the *African Charter on Human and People's Rights*: 'The family shall be the natural unit and basis of society', and the state has 'the duty to assist the family' and to assist all peoples (Art. 18, 20.3).

2.6 The *Haudenosaunee* (Iroquois) League

The confederacy among five (later six) *Haudenosaunee* (Iroquois) nations dates to between the twelfth and fifteenth centuries. Their oral constitution – The Great Law of Peace – specified that each nation elected delegates, or *sachems*, who dealt with internal affairs. The confederacy's Grand Council could not interfere with these affairs internal to each tribe, but could only handle specific matters of common concern such as war, peace, and treaty making. This conception of subsidiarity describes institutional design, and combined immunity for local units with joint authority for specific issues. The *Haudenosaunee* practice of granting the local units immunity apparently influenced Benjamin Franklin's and others' call for a union among the English colonies (Franklin 1904, Colden 1918–1937: 1: xv–xxiv, Fenton 1998). The oral tradition used the imagery of a bundle of five arrows tied together, which was later reused to symbolize the United States of America. Iris Marion Young explored this tradition to develop a theory of federalism that secures not only immunity for the local units but the centre's obligations to actively redress power imbalances (Young 2000, Levy 2007).[1]

2.7 Subsidiarity as Principle – in Constitutions

Finally, consider how subsidiarity occurs in constitutions and in their creation – often in federal states. Indeed, Bednar regards subsidiarity as the 'soul of federalism' (Bednar 2014: 231). A conception of subsidiarity may be a principle of institutional design when drafting or reforming constitutions. It may allocate authority or instruct a body how to use it. Note that subsidiarity in constitutions typically applies to the sub-state level concerning the tasks of the regions or municipalities, and seldom to the state versus supra-state bodies. This may be relevant for transposing subsidiarity to international law. We find various roles of subsidiarity for constitutions on all continents, next in rough chronological order.[2]

The Constitution of the United States of America enumerates federal powers, and Congress may also 'make all Laws which shall be necessary and proper for carrying into Execution' these federal powers (Article I. 8). The Ninth and Tenth Amendments acknowledge that the states and 'people' retain all other powers. 'The people' may indicate that subsidiarity 'goes all the way down' to persons or groups.

The 1848 Swiss Federal Constitution now explicitly states that subsidiarity must be observed both in the allocation and in the performance of state tasks (Art 5a).[3] It restricts central action to those tasks Cantons cannot perform, including those that require uniform regulation (Art. 43a (1)). The collective body that benefits from a public service must bear its costs but gets to decide on its nature (Art 43a.2,3). Subsidiarity applies to all three state levels – reflected in many cantons' constitutions. It leaves all unmentioned rights with the Cantons (Art. 3).

Canada's 1982 constitution and legal practice have elements not only of subsidiarity but also of the reverse. Its 'inverse enumerated powers doctrine' grants the federal government authority in all areas *not* reserved to the provinces (91). The Supreme Court's 'national concern' doctrine authorizes the federal government in certain cases: if the provinces are unable to address certain problems, if there are externalities wrought on other provinces, or if federal

[1] Thanks to Johan Olsthoorn for this reminder.
[2] Available at https://constituteproject.org/, cf. Gussen 2014, Cahill 2021.
[3] Thanks to Reto Walther for details.

action has comparative advantages (Bednar et al. 2001, Brouillet 2011: 613, Follesdal and Muniz-Fraticelli 2015, Da Silva 2023: 103). The Supreme Court reviews whether federal authorities honour subsidiarity. Note that central authorities must make equalization payments to ensure 'reasonably comparable levels of public services at reasonably comparable levels of taxation' (Art. 36(2)).

The 1917 Constitution of Mexico defines it as a 'pluricultural nation'. It grants indigenous peoples self-determination regarding political, economic, and cultural organization, limited by federal and state constitutions and by equal political rights for men and women (Art. 3). Article 115 specifies the tasks of municipal councils to secure communities' basic needs: water, public safety, and first response to emergencies. Article 124 reserves non-enumerated powers to the states.

The 2001 reform of the Constitution of Italy makes explicit mention of subsidiarity regarding assignment of administrative functions between municipalities, provinces, metropolitan cities, regions, or the state to guarantee uniform practice (Art. 118.1). It also imposes certain 'horizontal' subsidiary duties on the public bodies, namely to promote and presumably coordinate citizens' initiatives as individuals and as members of associations (Art. 118.4) The national Parliament can legislate only on enumerated subjects; the rest remain the jurisdiction of the regions (117.4). Some critics claim that the conception of subsidiarity at work is that 'public institutions intervene in social matters only when the private sector does not deal with them' (Durieux 2012: 23).

The German Basic Law of 1949 entrenches competences between the central and local levels of government, with an enumerated powers doctrine in a pattern of subsidiarity (Art. 30). Article 72 expresses subsidiarity – if not by that term – concerning the exercise of shared responsibilities in ways reminiscent of later EU treaties:

(1) In matters within concurrent legislative powers the Länder shall have power to legislate as long as, and to the extent that, the Bund does not exercise its right to legislate.
(2) The Bund shall have the right to legislate in these matters to the extent that a need for regulation by federal legislation exists because: (1) a matter cannot be effectively regulated by the legislation of individual Länder, or (2) the regulation of a matter by a Land law might prejudice the interests of other Länder or of the people as a whole, or (3) the maintenance of legal or economic unity, especially the maintenance of uniformity of living conditions beyond the territory of any one land, necessitates such regulation.

These conceptions of subsidiarity concern both the *allocation* and the *exercise* of authority – within limits required by distributive justice: There must be revenue sharing among the regions to guarantee the 'uniformity of living conditions in the federal territory' (Art. 106.3).

The German Constitution also mentions subsidiarity explicitly as one of several conditions on transfers of legal powers to the EU, which itself must be committed to subsidiarity, democracy, basic rights, and so on (Art. 23). This may affect which conception of subsidiarity – if any – should be transposed to international law.

Thailand's 1997 Constitution guides the state's discretion by subsidiarity considerations, requiring that it delegates 'powers to local governments for the purpose of autonomy and self-determination of local affairs' (Section 78).

The 1997 Constitution of South Africa expresses subsidiarity concerning the allocation of competences: 'The national government and provincial governments must assign to a municipality . . . the administration of a matter . . . which necessarily relates to local government, if – (a) that matter would most effectively be administered locally; and (b) the municipality has the capacity to administer it' (Art. 156.4, de Visser 2010). Note how subsidiarity here applies to several levels below the state.

Bolivia's 2009 Constitution requires that any creation or change of constituent territorial units must be governed by a long list of principles – unity, solidarity, gender equity, subsidiarity, and so on (Art. 270). So subsidiarity here explicitly guides the creation of units with authority. Dilemmas, and trade-offs among these principles are left unaddressed. Article 297 states an inverse enumerated powers doctrine.

Reform processes for Australia's Constitution in 2014–15 were to be guided by a White Paper which would include subsidiarity as the first of six principles guiding such reforms. The process stopped, though discussions of particular reforms continue (Evans 2014).

A Constitutional Convention in Chile elected in 2021 drafted a new Constitution. The draft was rejected in a 2022 referendum. One reason for the reform was the perception that the 1980 Constitution included *too much* or an *unacceptable* conception of subsidiarity. Critics claim that Articles 1 and 3 give the state a residual role, to *only* provide those services that individuals or the private sector cannot provide. The government has used subsidiarity arguments to privatize state companies and services, including education, health, social security, and pensions, ignoring obligations to secure equal opportunities. This abdication of the state to the market – what MacCormick might call 'market subsidiarity' – was an unacceptable case of 'subsidiarity that lacks solidarity' (MacCormick 1999: 152–153, Pizano 2020, TNI 2021).[4]

4 Thanks to Alejandra Mancilla for this example.

3 Elements of Subsidiarity

These brief sketches might fuel critics' concerns that the concept of subsidiarity is obscure. But charitable interpretations and clarity about ambivalences may help (van Kersbergen and Verbeek 2007: 224–225, Möllers 2011). Consider some salient differences among conceptions of subsidiarity (Kalkbrenner 1972, MacCormick 1999: 151–155 and Besson 2016 offer other categories). Which units and which subject matters does a conception of subsidiarity regulate? Does it regulate how to establish, allocate, or use authority? Which objectives and standards of comparative efficiency does it lay down? Who are authorized to apply the principle?

3.1 Domains of Application

A principle of subsidiarity may govern authority in certain issue areas, or more generally. Examples of the former include insistence that religion remains with sub-units, protected against interference by central authorities or even requiring support by them, or rulers' obligation to provide necessities to those in need according to Mencius, Aristotle, *zakat*, and *Ubuntu*. Other cases are protection against war as according to the Haudenosaunee, or the enumerated powers of central bodies in some constitutions.

3.2 Which Units: Vertical or Horizontal

'Vertical' conceptions of subsidiarity prioritize the smaller of nested territorial bodies, typically individuals and political units. Federal orders may entrench the allocation of authority, or central bodies are instructed to delegate some authority to more local actors, who then often act 'in the shadow' of revocation (Reinicke 1998: 89).

'Horizontal', 'functional', or 'non-territorial' conceptions of subsidiarity apply between such political bodies and *private* or *civil* bodies – functional social groups, markets, religious organizations, labour unions, or NGOs. Examples include the Italian Constitution (Art 118), the Swiss Constitution (Art. 6),[5] and that of Chile discussed earlier. The Confucian and Islamic (and, as we shall see, Catholic) accounts protect or promote private and religious bodies, or the 'natural' groups of family, churches, or guilds, imposing obligations on political authorities. Some arrangements combine vertical and horizontal subsidiarity, as seen in the Southern African Development Community Treaty 1992 Art. 23 (Von Staden 2016a: 48–49) and the Italian Constitution (Art 118, 1 and 4).

[5] Thanks to Reto Walther for this case of 'Gesellschaftspolitisches Subsidiaritätsprinzip'.

Horizontal subsidiarity in some sense may also apply *among branches of government* since individuals are closer to elected bodies than to independent judiciaries. Versions of horizontal subsidiarity thus support claims that the state should support corporatist and consociational arrangements (Millon-Delsol 1993, Bogaards 2023), or support market mechanisms rather than use state power directly. One rationale may be that such private or social bodies or the market are thought to leave more authority to the individual than the more coercive state bodies. This argument has flaws: recall that the Italian and Chilean Constitutions are criticized for permitting too many private and market arrangements. Intra-family domination and social death may surely also coerce individuals as much as the state.

Note that on this account, horizontal subsidiarity does not apply *among* private or civil bodies that are in some sense 'equidistant' from the more local unit – such as various civil bodies or sectors of international law. Horizontal subsidiarity instead concerns the relationship between these and a more distant or more coercive political body that should harmonize and promote them. Other authors apply the term 'horizontal subsidiarity' also to relations among bodies at the same level (Howse and Nicolaïdis 2003).

3.3 Establish, Allocate, or Use Authority

Conceptions of subsidiarity may apply to three main tasks: whether to *establish* institutions (Carozza 2003: 44, Gosepath 2005: 166, Barber 2018: 319); secondly to determine *which* authority a body or institution should have (Buchanan 2003, Rodden 2006, Zürn 2018: 79, Nine 2022: 197). In addition to such 'metajurisdictional' assignment or 'meta-authority' issues, subsidiarity may thirdly guide those who *use* authority. Courts and other bodies may also review such allocations or use, against a conception of subsidiarity.

Conceptions of subsidiarity differ concerning at least six related issues (Kapteyn 1991: 40–41, Mackenzie 1991, Neunreither 1993: 209, Delcamp et al. 1994: 12, Endo 1994, Von Staden 2016a: 31–32).

The first issue is that authorities may be required to *nudge* first or seek to elicit and *coordinate* local units' cooperation through organizations or by regulating markets, rather than to command or use coercive state authority directly.

A second distinction is between *negative* subsidiarity which prohibits central action, and *positive* subsidiarity which requires central authority to act in various ways under certain conditions. The Ganda society, Nahua culture, and Haudenosaunee league prohibited interference with local affairs. Several constitutions likewise prohibit central bodies from interfering in self-determining units except when authorized. Confucian thought combines the two, prohibiting interference unless the local community cannot secure inhabitants' needs, when the ruler *must* aid.

A third aspect is that the central authority may identify obligatory objectives but leave the choice of strategies to local units. The EU's directives differ in this way from its regulations. Mercosur tribunals and the ECtHR generally leave it to the states how to specify remedies (Von Staden 2016a: 35, Klumpp 2013: 251–253).

The fourth topic concerns the 'second order' authority to apply the principle of subsidiarity itself (Kumm 2006, Howse and Nicolaïdis 2016: 266, Barber 2018: 208). More local actors may apply subsidiarity 'from below', or central actors may apply it 'from the top' (Beer 1986: 402–411). The latter might happen by a specific 'subsidiarity assembly' (Latimer 2018b: 594, Blake and Gilman 2024: 130). Two contested issues are who decides which objectives the central body should pursue, and who assesses the comparative merits of actions by the local and central units. The aforementioned examples showed both alternatives. In Ganda society a dissatisfied tribe could withdraw from the central ruler, while the Constitution of South Africa grants the national and provincial governments the authority to apply subsidiarity vis-à-vis municipalities.

The fifth issue distinguishes between the use of subsidiarity by a body and a body that reviews this use. Such review may be done by political bodies that are arguably closer to the individual, or by judicial bodies. The EU combines these (Ch. 8.2). The review may itself be governed by some conception of subsidiarity – such as when the ECtHR grants states a 'margin of appreciation', or when the reviewing body only reviews a local unit's decision process rather than any outcome (Ch. 7.2).

The sixth topic concerns *sequencing* several bodies. Some versions of subsidiarity may require that more local actors act first and that central bodies serve a 'subsidiary' function when those local actors fail. The central unit may also be required to seek to strengthen the local unit before direct intervention. Recall how the Prophet Mohammad's *zakat* bolstered the recipient's capabilities. The UN Charter (Ch 7 Art. 52.2) requires conflicting states to first ask regional bodies for help before referring conflicts to the Security Council. In contrast the ECOWAS Court of Justice considers cases though local remedies have not been exhausted – but not cases that domestic courts have decided (Von Staden 2016a: 43–44, Bado 2019). So the central unit may *enable* the local unit, *remedy* its failures, or *substitute* if improvements are impossible (Chaplin 2014: 74, in Walther 2022: 31–32).

3.4 Aspects of Comparative Efficiency

Conceptions of subsidiarity allow central allocation of authority if necessary to secure objectives better than the local units can do alone or by voluntary cooperation. The central unit might provide such relative efficacy or effectiveness in various ways, for example, due to its better knowledge, ability, cost effectiveness, or higher willingness (Raz 2006). Conceptions of subsidiarity vary in at least five ways on these matters.

Who should have the authority to determine firstly the objectives, secondly how they should be 'balanced' against other objectives, and thirdly how well and efficiently they are secured by the local units compared to by the central body? There may be disagreement among and within the bodies on all these issues; recall the controversial balancing required in the Bolivian and Chilean constitutions (Ch 2.7). Section 9 considers such tensions between the two European courts.

Fourthly, what sort of *necessity* warrants central action? Must local units *be* unable, or only *likely* be *unable* to secure the objectives as effectively as the central authority? What if they are unwilling? The requisite coercive power and effects of central action can vary drastically.

Fifthly, must central authorities *actually* contribute, or only be *likely* to do so?

3.5 Immunity-Protecting and Person-Promoting Subsidiarity

This taxonomy allows a plethora of combinations. For our purposes it suffices to note two overlapping clusters. *Immunity-protecting* conceptions of subsidiarity have three features. They tend to uphold broad immunity for one level of social or political units from central body interference. Secondly, any obligations to other units require the local unit's free consent. Thirdly, they accept the de facto power and authority of an existing unit – family, city, region, or state – as sufficient for other units to treat it as legitimate. So the local unit's decisions preempt any reason the central unit has to intervene, be it to protect individuals within the local unit or to impose obligations on it to coordinate with others. Other conceptions of subsidiarity tend to be more *person-promoting*. They firstly apply 'all the way down' to the person (Neuman 2013). Secondly, they may support claims to authority not only of states or their local units, but also of municipalities (Weinstock 2014), cities (de-Shalit 2018, King and Blake 2018, Hirschl 2020) or non-territorial groups (Kymlicka 1995, De Schutter 2019, Da Silva 2023). Thirdly, the local unit's acceptable claims to authority, immunity, and veto are ultimately shaped and limited by how such allocations affect individuals both within and outside its territory.

4 Theories of Subsidiarity

A comprehensive review of historical theories of subsidiarity is far beyond this Element (cf. Millon-Delsol 1993). The following (re)constructions of some justifications only address some features to help us assess them and understand how subsidiarity may relate to international law. Several of them draw mainly on some – Western – contributors, but they support conceptions of subsidiarity found elsewhere. Several authors combine arguments of several different kinds. To illustrate: The anarchists Pierre Joseph Proudhon and Bakunin provided what we may regard as arguments for subsidiarity based on individuals' need for immunity, our need to recognize the freedom of others and contribute to society, and justified delegation of power only to solve common problems (Proudhon 1863 (1979), Bakunin 1882 (1970): 3–4, Prichard 2007: 641, Prichard 2022).

The following six arguments favour different conceptions of subsidiarity with varying domains, scopes, and objectives. They shed light on two concerns: individuals' interests and the account of just distribution. They firstly offer a conception of the person and of the proper relations among individuals and between them and various social associations. All are based on *normative individualism* in a broad sense, in that the ultimate bearers of value are individual human beings. Some but not all theories rely on such premises to yield standards for legitimate groups or institutions. They differ about which interests in a broad sense that count, and whether all individuals count as equals when it comes to standards of just distribution. With regard to individuals' interests, several accounts maintain that individuals' interests can only be secured within various forms of community, and several include other-regarding interests: obligations *towards others* – cf. *zakat* (2.4), and Wolff (4.5). Note that some justifications accommodate value pluralism: that individuals have conflicting conceptions of the good life and about which interests that merit public protection or support, and so on (Nagel 1987, Macedo 1993). With regard to issues of justice, some theories hold that one of the objectives that institutions should secure is just distribution among the persons and among the units. Some theories do not regard differences in background conditions and bargaining power as a matter of injustice, even when that affects the resulting distribution (Barry 1989, Weale 2020: 375). Others insist on minimum subsistence levels or even somewhat egalitarian distributions (*Rerum Novarum* (Leo XIII 1891 (1981) 22, 37; the German Constitution Art. 72.2).

The order of presentation of theories roughly reflects the decreasing immunity of local units they justify.

4.1 Immunity

4.1.1 Background: Althusius

Johannes Althusius (1557–1638) is hailed as the father of modern federalist thought. He developed a theory of subsidiarity influenced by French Huguenots and Calvinism to protect the religious associations in Emden against abuse of central power (Althusius 1603 (1995), Hueglin 1987, Hoetjes 1993, Endo 1994, Hueglin 1999).

Calvinists regarded Christianity as a personal matter of direct contact with God. At the same time, they endorsed political activism and theocratic oligarchy, insisting that the true mission of man and the state is to serve as an instrument of God in this world. A permanent minority in several states, Calvinists developed a doctrine of justified resistance against political rulers based on the right and duty of 'natural leaders' to resist tyranny. And local units should enjoy extensive immunity from interference by political bodies concerning internal matters, subordinate only to God's laws. This influenced the Dutch doctrine of 'souvereiniteit in eigen kring': 'Sovereignty within one's own circle'.

4.1.2 Conception of the Person and the State

Althusius – as Confucius, Ubuntu, and Aristotle – regarded humans as fundamentally dependent on others for the reliable provision of the requirements for a comfortable and full life. He did not use the term 'subsidiarity' but wrote that politics concerns *subsidia vitae* – the requirements of life. These can only be secured through aid and sharing in a symbiotic 'association' (*consociatio*) or polity (*politia*) (Politica I.4, Endo 1994: 631, Hueglin 1999: 152). Families, guilds, cities, provinces, and states are all justified in this way. The civil and political associations owe their legitimate claims to authority to how they enable individuals' holy lives. There is little, if any, concern whether individuals have an interest in personal autonomy.

These supportive tasks exhaust the rightful roles of these more central bodies. Each association claims autonomy within its own sphere against intervention by other associations – as in Ganda and *Nahua* (Aztek) governance. This immunity argument for subsidiarity resolves tensions between stability and pluralism by insisting on non-interference by the central unit. This accommodation of dissent and diversity prevailed over any theocratic concern to subordinate political powers to a particular religion – and vice versa.

On Althusius' view sovereignty resides collectively in the constituent cities and provinces which in turn grant a state legitimacy. Central government enjoys legitimacy only by delegation from the sovereign units of the union, and it has no power to address matters only of concern to lower levels, just as in Ganda and *Nahua*.

The role of the state is thus not to regulate a political sphere separate from the social communities but rather to coordinate and secure their common purposes in a symbiosis. The local units' interests must be served by the common action, as the local units see fit.

4.1.3 Characteristics of Althusian Subsidiarity

Althusius' conception of subsidiarity yields a weak centre, reminiscent of the Ganda society described earlier. Local units have extensive autonomy and a privileged position, with veto rights against any central unit action and even with a right to exit. True to the Calvinist roots, this version of subsidiarity holds that regions and associations may rebel and secede if the federation fails to satisfy its tasks – by their lights. It is the 'natural leaders' of local units who apply this principle of subsidiarity and assess effectiveness and necessity.

On Althusius' conception of subsidiarity the *common good* to be pursued by a central political unit is limited to those undertakings deemed by *every* local unit to be of their interest, compared to their status quo. This accommodates value pluralism across units. Full agreement on ends is not expected – which is why subsidiarity is required in the first place.

The Althusian conception is proscriptive and mainly concerned to secure *immunity*. This leaves little room for obligations of central units to assist local units, or to require central units to act beyond providing the 'requirements of life' they are authorized to provide.

Althusius' objective was to protect territorial non-political local units, but the arguments also apply between 'horizontal' consociational arrangements and the state (Lijphart 1968, Lijphart 1979, Lijphart 1995). Such non-territorial forms of federalism often lead to government by grand coalitions of groups with veto rights over matters important to them. The main task of the weak central state is to support the segments of society (Therborn 1989: 203, Wamba-dia-Wamba 1992). One example was the 'pillarized' social structure of the Netherlands. Each group – Catholic, Calvinist, Socialist – maintained separate, parallel institutions such as business corporations, churches, labour unions, schools, and healthcare organizations. This fits with the theological underpinnings of 'sovereignty within one's own circle' developed by the Dutch Reformed theologian and politician Abraham Kuyper (1837–1920) (Kuyper 1880, Cahill 2017).

4.1.4 Problems

At least three aspects of this account give pause. Althusius' account brackets the legitimacy of local units. Recognition of a local unit by others depends on its organizational resources, in effect entrenching powerful local units. Any 'internal' quality control is done by the 'natural leaders' of the local units, who are protected from assessment and intervention by a centre on any such contested grounds.

Althusius may be correct to fear centralized authorities, but the account seems to ignore other risks to individuals such as local tyrants, and any possible protection or support the centre might offer.

Thirdly, the units must agree on the centre's objectives and authority, bargaining from a base line of their current status quo. The resulting arrangements are often weak and unstable (Harrington 1656 (1992), Federalist 20). Coercive redistributive arrangements are off the agenda, rendering any inter-unit distributive justice as 'justice as mutual advantage' (Barry 1989).

These concerns are vividly illustrated by the South African practice of *apartheid* and separation into 'homelands'. Apartheid was long regarded as justified precisely by the tradition of 'sovereignty within one's own circle' with many of these characteristics, developed by Kuyper (Kuyper 1880, de Klerk 1975: 255–260, Kuyperus 1999, Weinberger 2014). But Kuyper's account relied on consent, and recognized the risks of local tyrants: the state should enable the various spheres, but also 'shield the individual from overbearance by his own group' (Kuyper 1880, Kuyper 1898 (2016), Baskwell 2006). But inter-unit distribution is not a matter of justice, and it is unclear who decides whether interference in a local unit is required.

This tradition suffers from an exclusive focus on certain risks, and brackets legitimacy standards for local units – yet grants them immunity from interference to protect group members or to secure obligations across units. This is implausible when some local units – associations or states – lack normative legitimacy, or when existing inter-unit inequities are due to prior injustice or otherwise violates appropriate standards of distributive justice. These flaws affect our assessment of immunity-protecting theories of subsidiarity – and possibly parts of international law, the topic of Part 2.

4.2 Non-domination

4.2.1 Background: Confederalism

Harking back at least to the American Anti-Federalists, the confederal tradition of political thought can offer a conception of subsidiarity where the liberty of local units is central. The liberty of concern is *non-domination* in the neo-republican sense (Skinner 1984, Pettit 1997). Political orders should protect the central interest of individuals to avoid being subject to the arbitrary will of anyone. Drawing on Montesquieu the Anti-Federalists argued that local units may cooperate for necessary defence from outside attacks. But to prevent despotism they should enjoy a veto against any central actions (Montesquieu 1748 (2002), Braybrooke 1983, Beer 1993: 219–243, Goodin 1996).

4.2.2 Conception of the Person and the State

This non-domination argument for subsidiarity primarily seeks to avoid tyranny by external threats and by central authorities, including imposition of their particular view of the good life. Note similarities to the Aztek and Haudenosaunee accounts earlier. This concern may stem from the interest in non-domination but also from the dangers of paternalistic justifications of state power, or from respect for pluralism of worldviews and conceptions of the good life. Several thinkers have argued thus, with varying acknowledgement of other interests and dangers (Humboldt 1850 (1993), Proudhon 1863 (1979), Hayek 1944 (1976), Cattaneo and Bobbio 1945 (2010), Berlin 1958, Weber 1972, Schumpeter 1976). Similar concerns appear to inform some critical theories of international law: Third World Approaches to International Law (TWAIL) and feminist legal thought (Gathii 2011, Otto 2016, Engle et al. 2022, Gathii 2022). These accounts often recognize other shared interests, for example, in securing means to meet basic needs, or for distributive justice. The argument from non-domination might also accommodate such interests, including background power imbalances within local units (Larmore 2001).

4.2.3 Characteristics of Subsidiarity

The non-domination argument yields a *proscriptive* interpretation of subsidiarity where local units enjoy veto powers. The local units can be geographical, as in the US debate concerning federalism, or functional. This argument appears to assume that the conception of the common good is mutual advantage from the status quo.

4.2.4 Problems

The non-domination argument suffers from weaknesses, some shared with arguments from immunity, and some pointed out by the American Federalists. The argument assumes that such immunity offers protection for individuals against tyranny. But it lacks quality control on how local authorities dominate or harm individuals. Federal arrangements do *not* reliably secure freedom. In the United States the immunity of units protected racists' freedom to uphold slavery in the southern states (Riker 1964: 145–155). Commitment to *everyone's* interest in protections against others' arbitrary discretion would rather require regulation of units at all levels – the hopes of some anarchists notwithstanding (Proudhon 1863, 1994). This is one reason why J. S. Mill shared Humboldt's wariness of state action, but still objected to Tocqueville's general support for subsidiarity (Humboldt 1850 (1993), Mill 1873 (1969): 116). Majorities in democracies may, of course, also be such tyrants (Federalist 10, Federalist 51, Beer 1993: 257).

Local unit immunity also ignores other risks to other interests. Madison and others warn that veto rights can block desired collective action unduly, so local units should sometimes be overruled for centralized action (Goodin 1992: 146–168). The veto power of permanent Security Council members may illustrate this.[6] This account also dismisses differences in background conditions and bargaining positions as irrelevant for distributive justice – unless the differences amount to domination. Of course, whether such implications are objections depends on our views of the common good and justice.

4.3 Freedom

4.3.1 Background: Immanuel Kant

Several of Immanuel Kant's arguments can justify a discernible conception of subsidiarity. Some aspects merit attention, not least due to his philosophy of international law and his influence on other thinkers (cf. Williams 1983, Herman 1993, Wood 1999, Ripstein 2009, Maliks 2014).

4.3.2 Conception of the Person and the State

For Kant central features of human beings are our equal dignity and our capacity to be our own masters, able to set and pursue our own ends for our own reasons. Such autonomy partly consists of *external* freedom – civil independence – secured by legal protection against constraints by other's arbitrary choice (Kant 1996, AA 6: 313–314). Legal rights are thus not just instrumental means to get other ends we desire, be it freedom, well-being, or happiness. Rather, external freedom is *constituted* by legal rights and duties that subject individuals to the rule of law instead of to arbitrary power.

Public authorities are legitimate insofar as they can be justified to individuals by providing the legal rights that constitute individuals' freedoms. The equal respect owed all requires laws that ensure independence so that no person is be bound by others more than he – or her – can in turn bind them. Individuals cannot obtain such independence without laws, so their equal freedom requires central state authority. For Kant, the public institutions at the domestic and the international levels are part of the same legal system, justified as necessary components of individuals' freedom in this sense. So domestic law cannot be assessed in abstraction from the international legal community of states.

A Kantian conception of subsidiarity can be traced in his arguments for the institution of marriage, the state, for and against colonialism, and for international law. Harmony within marriage requires centralized authority, allocated to the husband due to his superior 'capacity to promote the common interests of the household' (Kant 1996). Kant's 1780s defence of European colonialism is

[6] Thanks to Reto Walther for this example.

arguably also a subsidiarity argument (Flikschuh and Ypi 2014). Unlike white men, non-white men and women lacked mental capacities to be genuinely free. So they benefit from benevolent colonizers (Kant 1775 (2007), 1785 (2007), Eze 1998: 215). Kant later became a strong critic of colonialism and slavery, since colonial powers abused their authority (Kant 1795 (1996), Ripstein 2014). Whether he also changed his views about races is contested (Wood 2008: 7–9, Flikschuh and Ypi 2014, Kleingeld 2014: 64, Williams 2014, but cf. Maliks 2012).

We can also find subsidiarity arguments in Kant's arguments for domestic, international, and cosmopolitan law, still based on the premise of individual freedom as independence (Kant 1996: 455, 6: 311, Ripstein 2009, Flikschuh 2010). Domestic rule of law was insufficient: 'All men [*sic*] who can at all influence one another must belong to some civil constitution' (Kant 1795 (1996): 322, 8: 349). Within a nation all should comply with a constitution that secures their civil rights – the freedom worth securing. International right (*jus gentium*) should govern the relationship among states, and a constitution of cosmopolitan right (*jus cosmopoliticum*) should regulate the relation among individuals and other states. Such international constitutions secure the freedom of every state by securing peace or non-intervention, and by preventing threats and suspicion of tyranny (Kant 1795 (1996), 1784 (1996)).

Kant argued for the need for such common rules in a federation of peoples, and saw the risks of centralized authority. So forcible interference in other states would be an unjustified violation of the right of an independent people struggling with internal ills. Such a license would make the autonomy of all other states insecure (Kant 1795 (1996): 319, 8: 346). A centralized global authority with coercive power may turn despotic. The better alternative is an alliance or confederation which can be terminated at any time (Kant 1784 (1996), Kant 1996, 6: 344).

4.3.3 Characteristics of Subsidiarity

Kant's subsidiarity arguments concern allocation of authority but also which 'social ontology' we should have. Empires should be abolished, and new confederations should be established. These arguments might be seen to justify the EU and the ECHR and its Court (Habermas 2006, Tully 2008, Habermas 2012, Stone Sweet, and Ryan 2021).

These subsidiarity arguments see some institutions as having intrinsic value, since legal regulations constitute the sort of freedom Kant values. Hence his criticism of Grotius, Pufendorf, Vattel as mere 'sorry comforters' who ignored the need for legal force behind their moral code (Kant 1795 (1996)).

Kant's arguments support a conception of subsidiarity with a mix of proscriptive and prescriptive features. The state must respect individuals' civil and political rights so as to not interfere in their autonomous will formation. Some argue that this account also requires the state to facilitate individuals' ability to make autonomous decisions by ensuring their social and economic rights (Davies 2014, but Davies 2020). The state must also protect individuals from interference by third parties. Kant came to reject imperialism apparently on empirical grounds: the rulers abused their authority. Presumably patriarchal marriage would be similarly conditional, allowing interventions or exceptions when men abused their authority.

4.3.4 Problems

Kant's theories have met with both support and resistance relevant for these subsidiarity arguments. His focus on individuals' freedom only understood as legal protections of their independence seems unreasonably narrow. Other challenges concern the empirical assumptions, risk assessments, and implicit scope conditions of the arguments. Kant's defence of marriage is criticized as a 'mess' (Herman 1993) and 'an embarrassment to moral philosophers and philosophers of law alike' (Mendus 1992, Lloyd 1993: 65–70), for several reasons. The empirical premises about 'women's nature' are flawed. His reasoning is poor (Pateman 1988: 160–163): Why do families require one master, while such hierarchy is neither possible nor necessary among sovereign states? In response, Kant's egalitarianism, autonomy, and appreciation for legal regulation might ground a 'robust and liberating feminism' – if charitably shorn of misguided assumptions (Williams 1983: 179–181, Okin 1989, Schott 1997, Mosser 1999: 352, Cash 2002, Mikkola 2011, Varden 2017).

Kant's early endorsement of colonialism has been roundly criticized: it is empirically flawed concerning racial hierarchies, and has unresolved tensions between paternalism and autonomy. Others challenge Kant's ambivalence regarding risks of abuse of authority. He rejected international bodies due to risks of abuse and restrictions on states' immunity as domination. Yet he accepted imperialist interventions. His aversion to humanitarian intervention assumed complex empirical premises which would rather allow stringently regulated military intervention (Franceschet 2010, Williams 2012).

These criticisms illustrate the challenges to several subsidiarity arguments wrought by deep empirical contestations about individuals' and groups' abilities, interests, or objectives, about probabilities of risk, and about the relative effectiveness of feasible alternative allocations of authority.

4.4 Efficiency

4.4.1 Background: Fiscal Federalism

Economic theory justifies a conception of subsidiarity that grant units some powers, but less so than the immunity- and liberty-based accounts. According to fiscal federalism, the powers and burdens of creating 'public goods' should be placed with the populations that benefit from them, much as the Swiss federal Constitution (Art. 43a 2 and 3):

> For an economist, the principle of subsidiarity means that the production of public goods should be attributed to the level of government that has jurisdiction over the area in which that good is 'public.' (Padou-Schioppa 1995: 155)

Fiscal federalist arguments support decisions at a level close to the individuals when they share preferences, and only counsel more centralization when needed to secure such collective goods as free trade (Oates 1972: 11–12). There are at least two related arguments: preference maximization and epistemic considerations. Fiscal federal theory assumes that individuals have different preferences and that this heterogeneity is clustered geographically. Then local decision-makers are more likely to match the preferences of those affected and available policy alternatives (Musgrave 1959: 179–180, Oates 1972, Goodin 1992: 147–150). The match is further improved insofar as individuals can, and will, move among units to secure better fit (Tiebout 1956). Secondly, there is a risk that centralized authorities cannot respond adequately to information about heterogeneous preferences – a concern shared by the anarchist Bakunin (Federalist 10, (Hayek 1944 (1976), Bakunin 1971: 338)).

This preference for local units can sometimes be set aside for reasons of 'indivisibilities, economies of scale, externalities, and strategic requirements' (Padou-Schioppa 1995: 155). To assess the strength and limits of such efficiency arguments consider why and when local or central authorities contribute to provide 'public goods' in general – including 'club goods' among subsets of a population. We often assume that mechanisms to increase preference satisfaction are 'voluntary', such as markets, or individuals' choice to move to maximize their preferences. Exceptions exist, such as when coercive states help secure common interests in what are called 'public goods' or 'club goods' (Baumol 1952, Samuelson 1954). These are benefits (and avoidance of 'bads') whose consumption is *inexhaustible* – their use by some does not reduce that of others. This makes these goods attractive. But these goods are also *non-exclusive*: others' consumption cannot be prevented. Since it is irrational for any consumer to pay for them, it is irrational for producers to make and sell such public goods. So for these goods voluntary decentralized market exchanges fail to yield an 'optimal' distribution. A subsidiarity argument supports coercive political authority among that population to bring about the public good to secure their interests better.

The original theory of fiscal federalism assumes that preferences are fixed, and that institutions mainly affect their satisfaction. A 'second generation' of theories address cases where the institutions affect the preferences themselves, for example, creating new incentives (Qian and Weingast 1997, Oates 2005, Weingast 2014). One case is 'Hamilton's paradox' where officials of a smaller unit have incentives to overspend because they think that the central authority will bail them out (Rodden 2006). To avoid such externalities one solution is to centralize authority further – one explanation of the centralizing tendency of federations.

4.4.2 Conception of the Person and the State

This theory of subsidiarity focuses on individuals' preferences and takes them largely for given. The theory acknowledges value pluralism among individuals or groups – and assumes that the preferences vary systematically according to external or internal parameters. Geographical proximity or shared tastes and values within a group may justify the use of authority in everybody's interest, to secure Pareto improvements from their starting points which are taken for granted.

This theory assumes that coercive authorities have certain main legitimizing tasks, such as to secure public goods among members of a group, to prevent free riding, and to address externalities such as pollution that make outsiders worse off. It does not grant states a central role, nor support general claims to immunity such as sovereignty. To the contrary, this approach justifies multi-level and overlapping legal orders with separate authoritative bodies, each of which secures desired cooperation, even justifying new units to secure club goods. This subsidiarity should go 'all the way down'. The theory may also support placing powers with bodies above the state to manage externalities – for instance to regulate fishing or to prevent climate change. And the state is not guaranteed veto powers but may be overridden to ensure efficient co-ordination, to prevent free riding, or to prevent adverse effects on others (Samuelson 1954).

4.4.3 Characteristics of Subsidiarity

This account provides a prescriptive conception of subsidiarity that justifies and may require central action based on economic efficiency considerations. It guides allocation authority and may support new more centralized or decentralized units. An important issue not resolved by the theory itself is who should have the authority to apply such standards.

The account allows overlapping territorial and functional central units that are created and authorized according to the shared preferences of local units. So it justifies a 'neo-medievalist' world system of overlapping authority and multiple loyalties, asymmetrical or differential integration, which challenges order, transparency, and chains of accountability (Bull 1977: 264–276). One illustration may be the issue specific, yet overlapping, treaties of international law.

The theory does not protect the autonomy of units since states may be overruled for the sake of policies that better match the local units' preferences. Authority may be curtailed or moved to increase preference satisfaction of members of a unit, or to prevent harm to outsiders' preferences.

4.4.4 Problems

This theory of subsidiarity faces several challenges. One is its narrow focus. The 'public goods theory of the state' maintains that authorities' *main* task is to provide such public or club goods by deterring free riders (Baumol 1952: 57, Samuelson 1954, Samuelson 1955, Musgrave 1959, Olson 1965: 14, 38). To clarify: The account does not assume self-interested actors: it would support centralized authority to tax in support of those in need if members have such other-regarding preferences. These public and club goods are clearly important cases for collaboration. However, they are few.

Many observe that central authorities have other important tasks beyond policies that (almost) everyone prefers. Some proponents of the 'public good theory' concede this (Samuelson 1955: 355–356). The theory only applies to cases where *no* member is made worse off by the collective action at the various levels – securing a Pareto improvement among the members (Treisman 2007, in Latimer 2018a). But this account does not aspire to address questions of authority regarding *divisible* goods (Sen 1982). However, many rules or policies divide gains and burdens among members – indeed there may be few public goods in Samuelson's strict (or 'polar') sense. Unfortunately the label 'public goods' is often used more broadly, obscuring such important distributive questions (Samuelson 1955, Follesdal and Hix 2006, Follesdal 2021). The Pareto requirement also has peculiar implications. It prohibits central action that imposes any loss, however small, for any party, however few, for the benefit, however large, of others, however many, from their starting points – however unjust. So some constraints or 'quality control' on the domain of application of the theory seem necessary. To illustrate: it appears to justify slaveholders' or colonial powers' veto over the abolishment of slavery or colonialism because that makes them worse off.

A further challenge is that this argument supports too many allocations of authority, each of which increases preference satisfaction relative to the status quo. How might we choose among them? That becomes even more difficult when preferences are partly endogenous to the institutions – as the 'second generation' theories explore (cf. Da Silva 2023). Competing structures may coexist, creating fragmentation and conflict among authorities (Hooghe and Marks 2009, Nine 2022: 20, 197). Which criteria to apply, by whom, raises issues that appear beyond the reach of this account. We turn to one such case in Section 9.

Considered as a theory of subsidiarity we may question some of the premises of this account. The focus on economic utility and subjective preferences to the exclusion of other indices of individuals' well-being is problematic – especially when preferences are shaped by the institutions themselves (Cohen 1989). The approach does not address institutions that affect individuals' starting points and shape their aspirations and preferences. To illustrate: central and local governments can secure a match between policies and preferences by lowering individuals' expectations, or conflict entrepreneurs may fuel such mismatches to claim increased autonomy or secession from arrangements that secure 'public goods'.

The upshot of these observations and criticisms is not to dismiss the fiscal federalist theory of subsidiarity, but to underscore the need for further accounts and premises that answer these broader issues. Two alternatives appear next.

4.5 Perfectionist Justice

We here consider conceptions of subsidiarity that rest on a particular view of the person and of a natural social order, harking back at least to Thomas Aquinas (1225–74), inspired by Aristotle's justification of the city-state. The human good is to develop and realize one's own and others' potential and dignity. Individuals should thus 'perfect' their own abilities and develop their personality fully. This includes contributing to others' similar perfection. The following account sketches the Catholic tradition, noting some shared features with the views of Christian Wolff (1679–1754) and Pierre-Joseph Proudhon (1809–65).

4.5.1 Background: Catholic subsidiarity

Pope Leo XIII presented a Roman Catholic theory of subsidiarity in his 1891 encyclical *Rerum Novarum*. Pope Pius XI' 1931 encyclical *Quadragesimo Anno* – literally forty years later – claimed that:

> it is an injustice and at the same time a grave evil and a disturbance of right order, to transfer to the larger and higher collectivity functions which can be

> performed and provided for by lesser and subordinate bodies. Inasmuch as every social activity should, by its very nature, prove a help to members of the social body, it should never destroy or absorb them. (Pius XI 1931: 79)

Oswald von Nell-Breuning, a main contributor to *Quadragesimo Anno*, traced its conception of subsidiarity to German theologian and social philosopher Gustav Gundlach and the Italian Luigi Taparelli D'Azeglio (von Nell-Breuning 1962, 1986, Schwarte 1975: 41, in Cahill 2017).

Several claim that this conception of subsidiarity informs the conceptions in the European Union.

Pope Francis referred to subsidiarity in his 2020 response to the Covid-19 pandemic, insisting that the state must supply volunteers and families with sufficient resources to carry out their tasks.[7]

4.5.2 Conception of the Person and the State

The Catholic conception of subsidiarity assumes that the human good is to develop and realize one's own and others' potential. All persons are of equal worth yet may serve different roles within hierarchically ordered organizations according to their potential and interests. Starting with the individual, human societies, including secular and religious organizations, enjoy increasing levels of self-sufficiency. Thus, the province defends the city against enemies (*De Regno* (Aquinas 1266 (2002): I.2.4, cf. Aroney 2007: 186). Some note that this conception of subsidiarity has no general preference for a 'downward shift in responsibilities and powers' (Golemboski 2015: 285).

Individual's role and good – to live well – (Finnis 2016: 134–135) require active voluntary interaction with others. Persons develop their intrinsic dignity in voluntary associations (*Quadragesimo Anno*), which also assist those in need (*Rerum Novarum*). Similarly, Wolff argued that individuals should both 'perfect' their own abilities and contribute to others' similar perfection (Wolff 1736 (1996): 1, 213, Haakonssen 2012). Proudhon agreed: the full development of persons' personality required opportunities to contribute in various natural collectives (Proudhon 1863 (1979), Endo 2001: 14).

A conception of subsidiarity must be supplemented by a specification of such ends of each association as standards for the allocation and use of authority. Leaving that point aside, the state's role is limited to protect and respect the individuals and associations, including the positive role to provide aid. The

[7] www.catholicnewsagency.com/news/45936/pope-francis-subsidiarity-means-everyone-has-a-role-in-healing-society.e.

Confucian, Islamic, and *Ubuntu* accounts would agree. Wolff also argues that we have a *duty* to associate with others to assist those in need more effectively. The primary obligations fall on pre-political units such as the household, next of kin and friends. Only when the needy have no such support does the broader community have an obligation to assist them. State intervention is only *permitted* for individuals with 'no relatives or friends who could take care' of them (Wolff 1754: III, 2.1). For Wolff state measures are justified only insofar as they are the least costly way citizens honour these duties of public welfare and security (Wolff 1736 (1996): 229). Proudhon was even more sceptical, warning that state centralization created high risks of undue interference. Note the similarity with Confucian familial subsidiarity and Islam's *zakat*.

We see similar arguments in the Catholic theory of subsidiarity. *Rerum Novarum* had two aims: both to insist that the state must protect the poor against capitalistic exploitation and to protect the autonomy of the individual – and of the Catholic Church – against socialism and fascism (*Rerum Novarum* 36, 37, *Quadragesimo Anno*: 78, Van Til 2008: 615).

In his encyclical *Pacem in Terris* (1963: 137) Pope John XXIII extended this positive and horizontal conception of subsidiarity to a vertical, political application above the state, as did Pope Benedict XVI in *Caritas in Veritate* (Benedict XVI 2009: 57). Sovereign states must consent to establish new, albeit weak, global authorities to enable national authorities, citizens, and intermediate groups to solve global problems and secure global common goods.

4.5.3 Characteristics of Subsidiarity

The Catholic conception of subsidiarity encompasses both vertical and horizontal subsidiarity, negative and positive subsidiarity, and it applies above and below the state (Chaplin 2014). It regulates the establishment, allocation, and exercise of competence, and appears to place the authority to apply subsidiarity with the (non-state) Catholic Church.

The objectives include standards of distributive justice, especially towards those in need (*Summa Theologiae* II-II, q. 66, cited in *Rerum Novarum* 22). This justifies redistribution by the state, and constrains market exchanges to protect workers – including corporative structures such as labour unions (*Rerum Novarum* 22, 37, van Kersbergen and Verbeek 1994: 222, Van Til 2008: 614).

It allows for state intervention into civil society, with proscriptive and prescriptive elements. It requires support for local units yet prohibits state interventions which threaten the proper autonomy of individuals and associations.

This conception of subsidiarity preserves 'naturally occurring groups' (Cahill 2016: 121), but allows critical assessment of them, such as the state and at least some private and public organizations and arrangements. Popes used this account to criticize states for their failure to support local units, against fascist corporatism and poorly regulated markets, and to urge states to consent to global authorities necessary for global challenges (Hoetjes 1993: 133).

4.5.4 Problems

A central challenge to these perfectionist theories of subsidiarity concerns pluralism and disagreements about objectives. Wolff based his philosophical system on deductions 'from certain and unshakable principles by valid inference' (Wolff 1966: 33). He argued that the state should provide material goods and a criminal law, and cultivate the right religion, even ensure that individuals go to church (Wolff 1736 (1996): 421). Flaws or controversies regarding these starting points challenge the conclusions.

More deliberately pluralistic accounts of the 'natural' social order and the objective of human good might be compatible with this conception of subsidiarity, for instance, focussed on less controversial basic needs, standard risks and all-purpose means, or self realization (MacCormick 1999: 152). It might be possible to modify this, the Islamic, Confucian, or *Ubuntu* accounts to accommodate the appropriate interests of dissidents. Thus, Joseph Chan develops a 'moderate perfectionist' version of Confucianism explicitly for pluralist societies (Chan 2014). Pope Benedict XVI claimed that the Catholic understanding of subsidiarity is acceptable to believers and non-believers alike (Benedict XVI 2009: 57). But the particular specifications of the 'natural' 'family', 'dignity', and so forth rest on contested conceptions of the proper social order and specific ideals for human flourishing (Quadragesimo Anno, Pius XI 1931: 71). Disagreements limit the authority of any standards this conception can offer, be it concerning the role and powers of (heterosexual) families, of mothers, non-Catholic religions, labour unions, companies, the state, the EU, or the United Nations on such matters as fair wages or sexual and reproductive rights.

This is more problematic insofar as the Catholic account appears to allocate the authority to apply subsidiarity squarely with the Catholic Church. On some perfectionist accounts the risks of abusive states are even greater: Wolff does not licence individuals to protest illegitimate state authority, because they are unable or not empowered to do so (Wolff 1736 (1996): 434).

4.6 Legitimacy

4.6.1 Background: Social Contract Theory

We finally consider whether a liberal social contract theory in the Kantian tradition can justify or at least accommodate some conception of subsidiarity, and how well it responds to criticisms. The social contract tradition holds that a normatively legitimate social order must be justifiable to all affected individuals (Rawls 1971, Scanlon 1982, Waldron 1987, Hampton 1993, Barry 1995, Habermas 1996, Cahill 2016 offers a competing account). Whether

> principles for the design for social and political practices and institutions are justifiable . . . is given by determining what principles or practices could be agreed by parties to a hypothetical social contract in which the parties are rational. (Weale 2020: 3)

Authors in the social contract tradition insist on the centrality of the individual treated as political equals. This does not yield an obvious preference for allocating authority with units closer to the individuals, but we may discern at least two arguments for conceptions of subsidiarity that are consistent with this tradition, based on deliberation and on legitimate authority as elaborated by Josef Raz.

A principle of subsidiarity may foster public political discussions and bargaining beneficial to public deliberation and the character formation required to sustain a just political and legal order (Tocqueville 1945: 69). The focus on impacts, alleged benefits and losses, and comparative efficiency prompts a 'problem-solving' frame of mind, looking for shared values and agreement about the objectives of cooperation (Scharpf 1988). Some note similar benefits of proportionality tests: their 'disciplining and rationalizing effect on judicial decision-making', as 'conditions for constructive dialogues between courts' (Grimm 2007: 397, Stone Sweet and Andenas 2022: 28). However, many other public rules that do not express a preference for the local may foster such deliberate exercise of power and socialization towards others and the common good.

A stronger argument draws on accounts of legitimate authority by Neil MacCormick, Joseph Raz, and others (Raz 1986, MacCormick 1997, Raz 2006). Raz's 'service conception' holds that authorities' legitimate 'role and primary normal function is to serve the governed' (Raz 1986: 56). A central body might yield such services if it is wiser than the individual or the local unit, if it is less tainted by bias or weakness of will, avoids self-defeating collective action, is less costly for the subject, or is in a better position to secure 'what the individual has reason to but is in no position to achieve' (Raz 1986: 75). On Raz's account the reasons local units have are left open and may concern outcomes or processes, and be self-regarding or other regarding.

Such arguments support a rebuttable preference for individuals and more local authorities for two reasons. Firstly, MacCormick and others hold that individuals have an interest in being 'masters of their own destiny' (MacCormick 1997: 338–339). This may include having procedural influence over the social institutions that shape our values, goals, options, and expectations (Scanlon 1978: 102). Such influence furthers self-governance, avoids arbitrary control by others, and may provide a context for meaningful choices (Kymlicka 1995: 105). This interest is often secured better in local arrangements since fewer share control (Dahl and Tufte 1973).

Secondly, individuals may have interests that can only be secured by participating in local institutions. These may include opportunities to participate as voters and candidates in a democratic country, and the value of emotional and symbolic ties to local communities and even one's state. Subsidiarity secures such interests better by only allowing authority transfer to larger organizations when other objectives outweigh the losses to these values (Raz 2019: 79). Note that these subsidiarity arguments only apply to certain interests.

4.6.2 Conception of the Person and the State

Raz's focus on individuals' 'right reasons for actions' leaves open which interests individuals have beyond having influence over institutions. Subjective preferences will not always be decisive, and persons may be mistaken about what they have reason to do.

The account may accommodate value pluralism insofar as individuals may have reason to support common authorities that explicitly seek to accommodate disagreements about what individuals have reason to do. More plausible interests may include satisfaction of basic needs, protection from vulnerabilities, and all-purpose means such as education and income for pursuing one's conception of the good life.

4.6.3 Characteristics of Subsidiarity

These social contract arguments support a person-promoting conception of subsidiarity with a weak presumption for local units, and only in some sectors. It can address how to allocate and use authority, and support new institutions such as human rights bodies (Raz 2010: 42, Raz 2013).

This account may proscribe and prescribe central action and applies to other bodies than state including the EU (MacCormick 1995) and international law (Raz 2017). It may support intervention to protect individuals and minority cultures, duly cognizant of risks of abuse of such authority (Kymlicka 1995: 153[8]). Local units have weak claims to veto common actions or interventions lest they free ride on the cooperation of others, impose externalities on them, or block collective action in the common interests. So it offers weak and conditional

[8] I am grateful to Francois Boucher for this reminder.

support for sovereign states: 'political authorities are likely to have a more limited authority than the authority many, perhaps all of them, claim to have, and that people generally believe that they have' (Raz 2006: 1008).

4.6.4 Problems

The social contract tradition is controversial. Indeed, Raz was among it critics.[9] One objection was that when we regard wrong or unjust actions, appeals to a contract or reasonably rejectable rules do not explain or justify *why* we think so (Raz 2003: 356). In response some of these authors have other aims. The theories help account for what it *is* for an act to be unjust, and to help us decide what to think when we are uncertain – for instance, with regard to where to allocate authority and how to use it (Scanlon 1992: 23, Scanlon 1995, Weale, 2020: 405–407). Other critics challenge the alleged limited room within this tradition to value community (Fishkin 1986, Miller 1995), and its account of moral motivation as based on respect rather than empathy (but see Weale 2020). In partial defence, the arguments for subsidiarity offered might be independent on that tradition.

The 'theory' of subsidiarity is still severely limited in application and depends on complex empirical generalizations and counterfactuals, for example, concerning belonging, or the authority bundles required for various outcomes. And Raz's service conception of authority is contested (Hershovitz 2011, Viehoff 2011). The conception of subsidiarity seems to offer an easily rebuttable preference for the more local, in only some cases – and might at most structure arguments concerning the legitimate allocation of authority.

5 Modest Conclusions

These sketches of theories of subsidiarity do not allow strong conclusions, but six observations help respond to objections and yield implications for international law. Firstly, different accounts yield widely divergent conceptions of subsidiarity concerning who should have what sorts of authority in furtherance of a bewildering range of objectives.

Secondly, the Immunity and Non-domination theories suffer from their exclusive focus on the risk of domination or tyranny by central bodies, downplaying local tyrants and the need to pool authority for common objectives.

Thirdly, subsidiarity arguments can offer guidance only when ultimate objectives are given, such as specific conceptions of the good life. Wolff's and the Catholic conceptions have limited plausibility when there is not actual agreement among the individuals or local units.

[9] I am grateful to an anonymous reader who raised this concern.

Fourthly, some theories may endorse standards of distributive justice that apply within or among local units, be it unfair starting points, abuse, or unjust spoils. Some can also conclude that some local units are unjust. By such standards theories of Immunity, Non-domination, or Efficiency may perpetuate injustice within or across local units, be it slavery, apartheid, or unfair bargains. By their lights that might not be unjust.

Fifthly, person-promoting conceptions of subsidiarity appear less vulnerable to criticisms but also seem to offer weak support for a general preference for local authority. Any preference for the local depends heavily on empirical premises. They must also address disagreements about relevant interests and risks.

Finally, these conclusions might inform our interpretations and assessment of subsidiarity as used in international law – and indeed our assessment of the legitimacy of international law itself. Immunity-protecting justifications seem to match many state-centric features of international law, such as their broad immunity and veto powers. Yet these theories suffer major flaws. Person-promoting theories are more normatively plausible but appear less supportive of international law. They challenge the centrality of sovereign states in a multilevel social, political, or legal order. And states' immunity is less robust when interests of individuals inside or outside the borders are at stake. These appearances are deceptive. Person-promoting conceptions of subsidiarity may help explain, structure, justify, and reform many aspects of international law, including the domain of state sovereignty. Or so Part 2 argues.

PART II SUBSIDIARITY IN INTERNATIONAL LAW

What might be the current and future roles of subsidiarity in international law? One way to present and assess some answers is by considering the functions of a 'general principle of law', one source of international law. Several scholars argue that subsidiarity might serve as a general principle of law for European Union law (Castellarin 2019: 132) or for international law in general (Paulus 2008). Some detect an emerging pattern to this effect (Kumm 2009: 295); others have doubts at least in the shorter term (Carozza 2016, Jachtenfuchs and Krisch 2016: 20). The following claims may at most provide some philosophical arguments to these legal discussions.

6 Subsidiarity: A General Principle of Law?

The following argues that some person-promoting conceptions of subsidiarity satisfy the criteria of a general principle of law, one of the sources of international law listed in the ICJ Statute (Art. 38(1)c). General principles were recently discussed in three reports of the International Law Commission

(ILC Report 1, ILC Report 2, ILC Report 3). Examples include '*pacta sunt servanda*, good faith, the principles of lex *specialis* and *lex posterior*, respect for human dignity and elementary considerations of humanity' (ILC Report 3: 145).

General principles may be found in either national or international legal systems and may be transposed to the latter. This section argues that person-promoting conceptions of subsidiarity as they occur in national legal systems may be thus transposed, even though subsidiarity conception for international law appears to be immunity-preserving. Sections 7 and 8 consider subsidiarity as it appears in international legal systems.

General principles contribute to the 'coherence of the international legal system' when other rules of international law do not resolve a particular issue. General principles may guide law makers and judges when they interpret and complement these rules to fill gaps and avoid legal tensions; and they may serve 'as a basis for primary rights and obligations, as well as a basis for secondary and procedural rules' (ILC 2023 Draft Conclusion 10). The ILC reports note three desired forms of coherence, citing Andenas and Chiussi.

Principles may firstly be a *cohesive* force 'revealing and reinforcing the systemic nature of the system'. We next consider some sources of subsidiarity in national and international legal systems, and how subsidiarity may offer some system to international and domestic law.

Secondly, general principles may contribute to *inter-systemic coherence* 'between international law and domestic legal systems' (Andenas and Chiussi 2019: 10, emphasis added, Andenas et al. 2019, ILC Report: 143). Sections 7 and 8 explore how subsidiarity does that with regard to human rights, and in the EU.

Thirdly, general principles may also further *intra-systemic convergence*, 'avoiding or reducing fragmentation . . . . in different sub-fields of international law'. This fragmentation of international law stems from 'the rise of specialized rules and rule-systems that have no clear relationship to each other' (ILC Study Group 2006: 483). Some claim that this problem has got undue attention. Fragmentation may stimulate 'productive friction' towards a 'more responsive and effective international legal system' (Young 2012: 11). And actual inconsistencies are rare. However, the low frequency may partly be precisely due to harmonization by the ICJ and other courts (Fauchald and Nollkaemper 2012, Andenas 2015). And the growth of treaties and treaty bodies increases the likelihood of tensions. Be that as it may, Section 9 considers the limited contribution of subsidiarity for intra-systemic convergence by looking at two European legal orders with overlapping, yet different, objectives: the EU and the ECHR.

The rest of this section first identifies four interrelated forms of structure subsidiarity may provide to international law. We also find that the pedigree of person-promoting conceptions of subsidiarity is appropriate for a general principle. The section then addresses the conundrum that less justifiable immunity-protecting conceptions of subsidiarity appear to match better with international law than do person-promoting theories. This is a mistake: The latter may also support several state-centric features of international law.

6.1 Provide Order, Explanation, Interpretation, Justification?

Subsidiarity may serve as a 'structuring principle' for international law in many ways. It may firstly analytically *describe* various patterns, features of international law (Carozza 2003: 40, Neuman 2013: 363–364, but Carozza 2016: 54):

- States are immune to obligations of international law except when they consent.
- International law often supplements domestic legal order. The International Criminal Court (ICC) 'shall be complementary to national criminal jurisdictions' (Rome Statute 1998: Preamble, Art. 17, Bergsmo and Webb 2010).
- States often have international legal 'obligations of result' rather than 'obligation of means' (Schachter 1982: 349–350, Belgian language case (1968)). They can choose among measures that secure stated objectives. Other examples are 'common but differentiated responsibilities' (Paris Agreement on Climate Change Art. 2.2), and the EU's preference for 'directives' rather than 'regulations'.
- The UN Human Rights Covenants grant states positive subsidiary roles towards 'natural' family units – including necessary child protection against parents (ICCPR Art. 23(1), ICESCR Art. 10(1)).
- The ECtHR's 'fourth instance' doctrine limits its authority to correct domestic judicial errors, to only review conformity with the ECHR (Belgian linguistics case 1968, Schenk v. Switzerland 1988).
- The ECtHR and some other international courts and treaty bodies grant states some discretionary space – a *Margin of Appreciation* – to determine whether they have complied with their obligations.
- Conflicting states must request help from regional bodies before asking the Security Council, which in turn should engage regional enforcement bodies (UN Charter Art. 52(2), 53(1)).
- International courts usually only take cases where national remedies are exhausted.

- The *in dubio mitius* or 'restrictive' principle of interpretation requires international judges to interpret in ways that minimize constraints on state sovereignty (Merkouris 2017).

An immunity-protecting conception of subsidiarity appears to *describe* such features of international law very well. Such descriptions claim no causal or normative significance, nor does it entail that actors accept a principle of subsidiarity as giving them a reason to comply.

A practice we can describe as subsidiarity also contributes to the *causal* explanation of some features of international law. States agree treaties, and state practices identify customary international law and general principles of international law. States have de facto authority to apply arguments of subsidiarity – though not often by that name. This explains why, when, and how they agree to new treaties to compensate or supplement domestic law (Peters 2006).

Subsidiarity may *guide the interpretation* of international law. Judges or members of treaty bodies must often refrain from a strict review of how state legislation secures international obligations. Some also argue that these bodies should be guided by the *in dubio mitius* principle since states have only consented to minimal obligations.

Finally, arguments of subsidiarity might not only order, explain, and guide the interpretation of international law but also contribute to *justify* its claim to legitimate authority. A normatively convincing theory of subsidiarity may explain why some actors *should* take international law as a reason for action. Note that the inverse may also occur: If only *flawed* theories of subsidiarity support international law, this may challenge its alleged authority.

This justificatory function of subsidiarity may add value to the other three structuring functions. On their own, a theoretically coherent order, an explanation, or a particular mode of interpretation does not give actors reason to act accordingly. A normative theory of subsidiarity may offer such reasons, for why and when state consent creates international legal norms with legitimate authority. This may guide treaty makers and judges – and critics (Feichtner 2007: 17). Whether such claims *should* affect the interpretation of international law is a further, separate issue (Kammerhofer 2023). A theory of subsidiarity may, for instance, justify limits to the legitimating role of state consent in international law and the limits of sovereignty (Feichtner 2007, Kumm 2016: 264, Kumm 2009: 294). Several authors and sources appear to appeal to this justificatory function, regarding EU law (De Búrca 1999), international human rights law generally (Carozza 2003: 38), and specifically for the ECtHR (Protocol 15 to the ECHR); or to solve challenges of globalization and global governance (Slaughter 2000).

Does a principle of subsidiarity actually provide any such order for, and perhaps a justification of, international law? Subsidiarity seems to have the sources and contributions of general principles of law, may enhance the coherence among legal norms by guiding law makers' and judges' 'systemic interpretation' of international law when they fill gaps and avoid legal conflicts and tensions, both between international law and domestic law, and across different treaty regimes.

6.2 Sources and Transposition

Subsidiarity conceptions appear to have the appropriate sort of source for general principles of law. The ILC identifies two alternative pedigrees: from national legal systems or formed within the international legal system. The former arguably itself illustrates subsidiarity: some consensus of domestic legislations express general principles that restrain and guide international judges' discretion. Sections 7 and 8 look at cases of subsidiarity within the international legal system. Here we consider whether subsidiarity satisfy the two conditions for general principles derived from national legal systems. Firstly, candidate principles must be found in many jurisdictions, shown by an analysis that is 'wide and representative, including the different regions of the world' (ILC 2022a, Draft Conclusion 5). This Element does not aspire to a comprehensive analysis, but Sections 2 and 4 indicate that patterns, practices, and conceptions of subsidiarity – albeit perhaps few theories – are also found outside Europe. Subsidiarity or rules to that effect are found as a legal principle in constitutions on all continents. Note that the non-European exemplars of subsidiarity tend to be person-promoting rather than immunity-protecting.

The second requirement of a general principle derived from national legal systems is vague: it must be possible to *transpose* it to the international legal system. The principle must be 'compatible with that system' (Draft Conclusion 6, Mosler 1999: 517). Consider three challenges with regard to subsidiarity.

Firstly, some scholars note divergence between subsidiarity in international law and the Catholic domestic accounts. The latter is a case of horizontal subsidiarity between pre-existing private bodies and public authorities (Brennan 2014, Golemboski 2015, Cahill 2017: 213). They contrast this to international law where subsidiarity only concerns public bodies, some which are deliberately created by states. In response, I submit that this contrast is overdrawn. Even some popes have applied the Catholic conception vertically among only political bodies, and in support of creating new supranational authorities (John XXIII 1963: 137, Benedict XVI 2009: 57).

A second, more fundamental, challenge is that the aspects of international law canvassed earlier appear to only fit immunity-protecting conceptions. In contrast, many of the occurrences in domestic practices and constitution are not immunity-protecting but person-promoting. So immunity-protecting conceptions might even depart from the 'ordinary meaning' of the term 'as recognized by civilized nations' (Vienna Convention on the Law of Treaties 1969a: 31.1, 32.a).

Thirdly, from the perspective of normative political theory we should be concerned if it is only normatively problematic immunity-protecting conceptions of subsidiarity that can be transposed to international law. This may reduce the legitimacy of the latter.

In response, many of the relevant features of international law canvassed earlier can also be justified by more plausible person-promoting conceptions of subsidiarity. And those aspects of international law that fit less well are contested. Consider now these features again.

6.3 Role of Consent

The immunity-protecting theory of subsidiarity seems a better fit with the sources of international law, not least according to 'international legal positivist' voluntarist accounts. These claim that states explicitly or tacitly consent to *all* sources of international law, adducing the *Lotus* case of the Permanent Court of International Justice (PCIJ 1927: 18, Simma and Paulus 1999: 305, d'Aspremont 2022: 66–67, Besson 2009: 360). In response note that others hold that state consent is less central (Peters 2006: 579, Besson 2011: 51). Several non-treaty-based sources bind states regardless of their consent, including *jus cogens* and international custom (Crawford 2012: 123–124). States can be bound by treaties even when they are coerced to sign (VCLT Art. 38, 53, 75). Indeed, many of these norms are person-promoting, including those human rights that are now customary rules of international law (Pellet 2000: 38). Furthermore, many immunity-protecting features only occur within domains delineated by what we may regard as person-promoting constraints. For instance, *jus cogens* norms limit what states can agree to with binding effect. In contrast the more justifiable person-promoting conceptions of subsidiarity may accommodate such non-consent-based rules. They may also justify laments about states' broad discretion and immunity in public international law (Donnelly 2003, Krisch 2014).

6.4 Only Supplement Domestic Law?

One role of international law is to *supplement* domestic law, for example, to compensate for flaws wrought by globalization (Peters 2006). To secure state sovereignty in this way may appear to rest on an immunity-protecting conception of subsidiarity. In response, the relationship between sovereign states and international law is more complex than this one role. International law even partly determines and specifies state sovereignty (Pellet 2000: 37). For instance, states' authority to enter treaties with binding legal effects is created or specified by international law (VCLT Part 2). Person-promoting conceptions of subsidiarity may also justify these roles of international law, and may guide debates about how to delineate such domains of state sovereignty (Kumm 2009: 291, Kumm 2016: 241). Also on such accounts international law may compensate weaknesses of domestic law.

6.5 Exhaustion of Local Remedies

International law frequently requires parties to exhaust national legal remedies before turning to regional or international authorities (Adler 1990). Not only may this be more efficient, but it also safeguards state sovereignty, consistent with immunity-protecting sovereignty. In response, firstly the pattern is more nuanced, often allowing exceptions if such local remedies will not be effective (Couronne and Maurel 2019). And some treaties lack this requirement – sometimes because states may prefer *alternatives* to slow or untrustworthy domestic arrangements. Examples include the ECOWAS' Court of Justice, and tribunals under the International Centre for Settlement of Investment Disputes (ICSID (Peters 1997, Von Staden 2012: 1036, Brauch 2017, Bado 2019). Secondly, person-promoting conceptions of subsidiarity may also accept these rationales and limits on the presumption, as well as arguments based on respect for democratic decisions – as for the ECtHR.

6.6 *In Dubio Mitius*

In dubio mitius – the doctrine of 'restrictive interpretation in favour of state sovereignty' – holds that treaties should generally be interpreted to minimize states' obligations (Advisory Opinion 1925, Crema 2010: 685, Orakhelashvili 2003). This appears more consistent with immunity-protecting conceptions of subsidiarity. In response, firstly this principle is difficult to reconcile with treaties that states intended should restrict their regulatory options in areas such as human rights or foreign investments. Thus, the ECtHR generally rejects such immunity-protecting interpretations of treaties or exceptions (Golder *v.* UK 1972: 36, Klass *v.* Germany 1978: 42). Secondly, many note a shift away from in *dubio mitius* due to developments of international law and rules of its interpretation (Crema 2010). It is absent from the VCLT, where interpretations instead focus on the object and purpose of the specific treaty (Art. 31), assuming that parties intend the treaty to be effective (Jennings and Watts 1992: 1278, Merkouris 2017). Person-promoting conceptions of subsidiarity support this trend while acknowledging the need to curb the discretion of international judges.

6.7 Dethroning the State in International Law

A final response to the apparent mismatch between international law and person-promoting conceptions of subsidiarity is that international law's alleged exclusive focus on states may be overstated and is challenged. Several argue that states are not the 'ultimate units of concern' (Pavel 2014: 1–56). Thus, *jus cogens* norms show 'that the "system" of sovereign States is not an aim in itself, but a means for the safeguard of human values and interests' (Paulus 2005: 332). Likewise, the ICJ's Barcelona Traction case holds that obligations *erga omnes* derive from 'the principles and rules concerning the *basic rights of the human person*, including protection from ... racial discrimination' (cf. Crawford 2014: 485, emphasis added).

While the primary *subjects* of international law may remain states, their *objectives* and that of international law increasingly express a commitment to normative individualism (Pellet 2000: 6, UN High Level Panel 2004: 4, Peters 2009, Criddle and Fox-Decent 2016). This fits with person-promoting conceptions of subsidiarity. Several authors mentioned provide normative justifications in support of such conceptions, challenging presumptions of states' immunity and veto.

One conclusion is that transposition of person-promoting conceptions of subsidiarity from domestic legal orders is not precluded because any conception of subsidiarity for international law must be immunity-preserving. Sections 7 and 8 consider the other pedigree for a general principle: its occurrence in international law.

7 Inter-systemic Coherence: Human Rights and State Sovereignty

Conceptions of subsidiarity may promote inter-systemic coherence between international and domestic legal orders. One striking aspect is that the result may be very different depending on the conception of subsidiarity and the objectives that inform the adjustments. We see this in the different ways regional human rights norms may interface with domestic authorities.

Sovereign states often commit to treat individuals under their jurisdiction in certain ways by signing human rights treaties. States even sometimes allow international review and adjudication of their compliance with these treaties. Why do they do this? One prominent explanation is that states bind themselves to enhance their credibility towards various actors (Alter 2008b: 49). 'Self'-binding is somewhat misleading since governments mainly seek to bind their successors to respect human rights (Moravcsik 1995; Elster 2000: 92). Leaving the objectives aside, human rights violations become a matter of 'international concern' (Beitz 2009). And such commitments may mobilize various branches of government and 'compliance constituencies' in civil society to respect and protect human rights (Moravcsik 1995, Dai 2005, Alter 2008a).

What authority should human rights treaties and treaty bodies enjoy, and how should they exercise it?

Can subsidiarity help delineate the appropriate scope and processes of such deference towards states? Politicians in Argentina, Brazil, Colombia, Paraguay, and Chile seemed to think so when they objected to what they saw as a too invasive role of the Inter-American Court of Human Rights (IACtHR). They called for more subsidiarity in defence of state sovereignty (Argentina et al. 2019). Some deference to states may be warranted due to the different social and natural conditions, cultures, and policy trade-offs within the different states which an international body is ignorant about. Yet to leave adjudication of compliance completely to each state will not only render the treaty too ineffective, but also incapable of instilling trustworthiness among various constituencies. We see that by how immunity-protecting and person-promoting conceptions of subsidiarity yield quite different recommendations. Two cases are the Human Rights Declaration of ASEAN and that of the ECHR and the ECtHR, respectively.

7.1 Association of Southeast Asian Nations (ASEAN)

The ASEAN 2009 Intergovernmental Commission on Human Rights and the 2012 Human Rights Declaration illustrate immunity-protecting subsidiarity.

At the time of the founding of the ASEAN in 1967 the aim was to bolster the five relatively weak states through sovereignty reinforcement (Preamble 1967 ASEAN Declaration). By 2007 the then ten member states agreed to a Charter which underscores sovereignty and non-interference into the internal affairs of other states (ASEAN 2007, Ginsburg 2020: 244). Member states shall avoid external and intra-regional conflicts and reduce risks that larger members would dominate the smaller (Goh 2003, Acharya and Stubbs 2008, Saul et al. 2011, Beckman et al. 2016). Note the similarity to the Baganda, Haudenosaunee, and Althusian accounts of subsidiarity.

Their concern for 'the Asian way' of non-interference notwithstanding, the ASEAN states agreed to a Human Rights Commission and Declaration. One reason might have been to provide external legitimacy to the ASEAN (Duxbury and Tan 2019: 344). The Declaration might also help avoid conflicts stemming from more regionally migrant workers and from increased interdependence within the ASEAN Economic Community.

Subsidiarity is not mentioned in the Declaration, but it seems an apt description of the ASEAN human rights regime. The only form of international concern shall be in the form of cooperation, but no judicial or political review. To the contrary, use of the Declaration must respect principles of non-confrontation and non-politicization (Art. 9). The same holds for mandate and activities of the Intergovernmental Commission on Human Rights.

Observers note that even such a weak Declaration apparently modified ASEAN's respect for non-interference. ASEAN expressed concern in 2016 about the plight of the Rohingya minority in Myanmar (Duxbury and Tan 2019: 340–341). But UN bodies, experts, and civil society groups[10] denounced what we may describe as the immunity-protecting subsidiarity elements of the Declaration. The interests and immunity of state governments take priority over the interests of individuals. *All* human rights must be 'balanced with the performance of corresponding duties' (Art. 6); and are limited by laws that secure such objectives as national security, public safety, public morality, and the general welfare (Art. 8). So the state may limit or balance all human rights against other objectives and values. As we will see next, other regional human rights conventions also allow some balancing, but only regarding some rights against a more limited set of objectives, and subject to international review. The ASEAN human rights declaration therefore provides neither much human rights protection nor trust in the governments' human rights commitments.

We see that immunity-protecting conceptions of subsidiarity may help resolve tensions between regional human rights norms and state sovereignty, in favour of states' immunity and broad discretion. But the ASEAN Human Rights Declaration and Commission appear to contribute little to secure the objective of human rights against the will of any ASEAN state. So the legitimacy of the Declaration may be at stake.

7.2 The ECtHR's Doctrine of a Margin of Appreciation – Subsidiarity or Submission?

The ECtHR sometimes defers to the respondent state's own court's judgement of whether the state is in compliance with the ECHR. This 'Margin of Appreciation Doctrine' ('Doctrine') resolves some inter-systemic tensions between the states' sovereignty and their Convention obligations, and alleviates the 'perceived conflict between international human rights protection and

[10] www.un.org/apps/news/story.asp?NewsID=43536#.UgzNzpIwfng.www.un.org/apps/news/story.asp?NewsID=43520&Cr=human+rights&Cr1=#.UgzO6pIwfng.www.hrw.org/news/2012/11/19/civil-society-denounces-adoption-flawed-asean-human-rights-declaration.

democracy' (Arai-Takahashi 2001, Arai-Takahashi 2013, Laffranque 2015: 43, cf. Bates 2016, Walther 2022, Walther 2025).

The Doctrine was created by the Court itself, and harks back to a 1958 Cyprus case. The states recently included this Doctrine in the Preamble to the ECHR, explicitly as an expression of subsidiarity:

> Affirming that the High Contracting Parties, in accordance with the principle of subsidiarity, have the primary responsibility to secure the rights and freedoms defined in this Convention and the Protocols thereto, and that in doing so they enjoy a margin of appreciation, subject to the supervisory jurisdiction of the European Court of Human Rights established by this Convention.

Some find similar doctrines by other international courts, and suggest that it should be copied elsewhere (Shany 2005). However, critics warn against export (Trindade 2006). Why?

Some critics regard the label 'doctrine' an unduly charitable misnomer. Its vagueness creates legal uncertainty and leaves judges too much discretion (Brauch 2005: 125, Macklem 2006, Lester 2009, Arai-Takahashi 2013, z v. Finland 1997, Judge De Meyer partly dissenting). More fundamentally, this Doctrine challenges the very raison d'etre of the Court (Benvenisti 1999, Sweeney 2005, del Moral 2006: 614, Carter 2008, Kratochvil 2011, Spielmann 2012). The Court thereby abdicates from its task to protect the ECHR and to be its ultimate interpreter (Yourow 1996: 181, Benvenisti 1999, Hunt et al. 1999, Letsas 2006, Kratochvil 2011).

Against these objections, a person-promoting conception of subsidiarity can defend a charitably reconstructed Doctrine which prevents human rights abuses whilst deferring appropriately to well-functioning democratic rule. The explicit role of the ECtHR is to *assist* states in securing 'the universal and effective recognition and observance of the Rights therein' (ECHR Preamble) by supplementing and strengthening the protection offered by domestic judiciaries. This role expresses a positive conception of subsidiarity which seems compatible with granting the state a margin of appreciation when the domestic courts are *at least as well suited and trustworthy* as the ECtHR to determine whether there is a breach (Brems 2019). That condition yields several implications, many of which match the – admittedly vague – Practice.

The ECtHR holds that states may be granted a margin of appreciation in at least three main issue areas: (1) 'Balancing' certain human rights – to private life, religion, expression etc. – against urgent issues – emergencies or public safety, and so on (Art. 8, 9, 10). (2) 'Balancing' among different human rights such as freedom of expression (Art. 10) vs privacy (Art. 8). (3) Applying the ECHR to the specific circumstances, values, and traditions of a state.

The Court sometimes holds that domestic authorities are in principle 'better placed' than an international court to make such assessments (Hatton v. UK 2003: 634), or because they are 'in direct and continuous contact with the vital forces of their countries' (*Handyside v. UK*). A domestic court may indeed have more local knowledge in these three areas. But the risk of its (un)intentional misjudgement may be too high for certain non-derogable rights – to life (Art. 2), and against torture (Art. 3), slavery or forced labour (Art. 4). This matches the Practice.[11]

Note that some 'balancing' among human rights does not render human rights protection *less stringent*, so deference on this point does not clearly entail a lower protection of human rights. Within some range of 'balancing', if that choice emerges from a proper deliberative democratic process – a 'vital force', – there would arguably be little grounds for the Court to review the outcome.

From this perspective the ECtHR should not allow a margin of appreciation for freedom of expression and other rights required for well-functioning democratic decision-making. Indeed, this appears to be the pattern (*Handyside v. UK* para 49, Observer *v.* UK, partly dissenting opinion of Judge Pekkanen). And the *ability* of domestic courts to adjudicate, or for domestic authorities to strike a balance based on democratic deliberation, is not enough. The ECtHR should check that the national authorities have in fact considered less restrictive alternatives and any negative impact on human rights. Under these conditions the ECtHR arguably is unlikely to provide a better assessment of violations of the Convention than domestic independent judiciaries.

On this line of reasoning the ECtHR should require as a condition for granting a margin of appreciation evidence that the respondent state has actually undertaken a good faith proportionality test to the satisfaction of its independent domestic judiciary. Otherwise, there would be no democratic deliberative decision worth for the ECtHR to defer to. There is some – but inconsistent – evidence of an explicit practice to this effect (Lindheim *v.* Norway: 85, Spano 2018, but Schalk and Kopf *v.* Austria). And if the ECtHR checks whether the state has carried out such a 'proportionality test', the Court may also help the population determine that their government has done so. This requirement may also nudge states to more careful proportionality testing – in effect another supportive subsidiary effort by the ECtHR.

These arguments support the recent inclusion of a Margin of appreciation in the Preamble of the ECHR, based on a person-promoting conception of subsidiarity. It is a means for the ECtHR to monitor and promote member states'

---

[11] M.C. v. Bulgaria 2003b, Budayeva v. Russia 2008, and Beganovic v. Croatia 2009a may be exceptions. Thanks to Oddný Mjöll Arnardóttir for these references.

human rights compliance, while sometimes being deferential in the particular cases when the domestic democratic process warrants. These conditions may also render the Doctrine suitable in other regions (Follesdal 2017).

Critics might still object that this is a smokescreen, and that the Doctrine is really justified by an immunity-protecting conception of subsidiarity. After all, the ECHR Preamble only mentions states, not individuals. In response, note first that a person-promoting theory of subsidiarity may also justify the role of the ECtHR, as indicated previously. Secondly, even though the Subsidiarity text of the Preamble only mentions states, the scope conditions for this conception are person-promoting: All States Parties are explicitly committed to 'secure to everyone within their jurisdiction the rights and freedoms . . . ' (Preamble). And since the conception of subsidiarity only applies among states thus committed, its scope conditions make it unnecessary to repeat the focus on individuals. The States Parties also appeal to a conception of subsidiarity that applies below the state when they insist that the states must support human rights stakeholders in civil society (Council of Europe 2018: 16–17).

To conclude: subsidiarity may contribute to inter-systemic coherence with regard to international human rights law. The two cases of ASEAN and of the ECtHR show that the choice of more immunity-protecting or more person-promoting conceptions has drastic implications for the contents of the more coherent system of norms. The choice between them requires an authoritative ordering between the objectives of human rights and sovereignty – which subsidiarity itself does not provide.

8 Inter-systemic Coherence: Subsidiarity in the European Union

Treaties serve several other roles than those provided by the human rights treaties discussed in Section 7. These importantly let governments bind other states but also their own successors to human rights compliance. Even if not all other states sign up and comply, a signatory may benefit by a reputation of being a human rights committed government. States commit to many other treaties primarily in order to bind *other* states, and general compliance is crucial. One example is free trade, where treaties provide crucial services by preventing protectionist measures, tariffs, and 'beggar thy neighbour' policies. These are central objectives for the European Union and the World Trade Organization (WTO) whose courts and tribunals monitor and adjudicate questions about compliance. Person-promoting theories of subsidiarity may apply in two ways regarding the European Union to promote inter-systemic coherence: concerning the subsidiary role *of* the EU and *within* the EU treaties specifying how the EU should defer to states. Though some claim that less deference is appropriate in these cases than in the 'self binding' arrangements, subsidiarity does play a role (Shany 2005: 920–921, von Staden 2016b). Consider first a brief history and then the practice of subsidiarity (in-depth studies include Fabbrini 2018).

8.1 A brief History of Subsidiarity in the European Union

Over centuries several philosophers have called for a (con)federation of European states (Bakunin 1867 (1972), Kant 1991). The conception of the European Union is still often held dated to 1950. Then France's foreign minister, the Roman Catholic Robert Schuman, argued for a new common authority among European states to pool coal and steel production in order to secure peace among them (Schuman 1950). Six states agreed, and later expanded their cooperation to other sectors in the 1957 Rome treaty. A pattern of subsidiarity is visible at this birth, even though the term 'subsidiarity' was absent. Many still trace a trajectory from the Catholic conception developed in German social thought, together with Mounier's theory of *Personalism* in France, inspired by Proudhon (Proudhon 1863 (1979), Mounier 1957, Haas 1958: 115, Delors 1989, Marquardt 1994, Burgess 2000, Prodi 2000, Barber 2005, Barroche 2007).

The term 'subsidiarity' seems to appear first in EU's legal documents in 1975, due to Altiero Spinelli's authorship of the European Commission's response to the Tindemans report on the 'European Union' (Tindemans 1976). He clearly saw a need to alleviate fears of centralization: the

> European Union is not to give birth to a centralizing super-state. Consequently, and in accordance with the *principe de subsidiarité*, the Union will be given responsibility only for those matters which the Member States are no longer capable of dealing with efficiently … the Union must be given extensive enough competency for its cohesion to be ensured. (European Commission 1975 Para 12)

At the same time, when 'asking how consistency can be secured between action by the Union and action by the Member States. The answer is that Union law takes precedence over national law' (Para 14).

Altiero Spinelli included the term 'subsidiarity' in the draft treaty establishing the European Union' (Bieber et al. 1985, 306–329, Endo 1994, Ch. 3). And 'subsidiarity' appeared in the 1986 Single European Act (SEA) albeit only for environmental issues. One main reason was to ameliorate fears of rampant European integration, in the UK and among European regions, especially the 16 German Länder (Golub 1996, Borries and Hauschild 1999: 371, Pollack 2002: 519). Subsidiarity became more central and explicit in later treaties, first in the 1992 Maastricht Treaty on European Union (van Kersbergen and Verbeek 1994,

Craig 2012). In the Preamble subsidiarity appears to guide allocation of authority while Art. 3(b) concerns its use:

> ... *Resolved* to continue the process of creating an ever closer union among the peoples of Europe, in which decisions are taken as closely as possible to the citizen in accordance with the principle of subsidiarity.

The 2007 Lisbon Treaty version of subsidiarity explicitly mentions the regions:

> Under the principle of subsidiarity, in areas which do not fall within its exclusive competence, the Union shall act only if and in so far as the objectives of the proposed action cannot be sufficiently achieved by the Member States, *either at central level or at regional and local level,* but can rather, by reason of the scale or effects of the proposed action, be better achieved at Union level. (emphasis added)

This *Lisbon* subsidiarity only applies where the Union shares competence with the member states. A Protocol specifies how to operationalize this (Amsterdam Treaty 1997, Lisbon 2007): EU bodies must choose the form of action that interferes least with national law, such as directives rather than regulations, leaving as much scope for national decisions as possible consistent with the aims of the measure. This was later deleted (COM 2010 (547) final, 3, cf. Lööw 2013: 18). Legislative proposals should be accompanied by reasons why the objective could be 'better achieved' at the Community level, 'by qualitative and, wherever possible, quantitative indicators' (1997a, Art. 5).

Subsidiarity also occurs in the *Charter of Fundamental Rights of the European Union*, in force since 2007. The EU treaties originally did not explicitly require the EU to respect human rights. But starting in 1969, the ECJ read human rights into the treaties as general principles of law, and reviewed Community action against them (Stauder *v.* Ulm, Internationale Handelsgesellschaft: 4, Weiler 1991: 15). The Member States confirmed this change in later treaties and in the Charter in 2000. Subsidiarity is mentioned in the Preamble, and in Article 51(1)

> The provisions of this Charter are addressed to the institutions and bodies of the Union with due regard for the principle of subsidiarity and to the Member States only when they are implementing Union law.

The Charter only applies to EU law, while the rest of Member States' legislation is already subject to the ECHR and domestic human rights protections. The importance of who has authority to apply a conception of subsidiarity is evident in disagreements about whether the Charter only applies where European law leaves no room for national discretion, where the CJEU and the German Constitutional

Court disagree (Paulus 2013: 179). This affects whether subsidiarity constrains or promotes centralization (Riker 1964: 210, 'de Tocqueville 1835 (1969): 296, Lemco 1991, Bednar 2008, Dardanelli et al. 2018).

8.2 EU Subsidiarity in Practice

Why is the Lisbon subsidiarity principle important, and how does it work in practice? The EU has a vast range of objectives – TEU Art. 3 specifies at least fifty-one, including free movement of persons, an internal market; solidarity among Member States, and human rights. And EU law must respect and promote the rights listed in the Charter. How should the EU 'balance' or prioritize among these objectives, and who should have the authority to do so?

The treaty gives clear priority to ensure an internal market with 'the free movement of goods, persons, services and capital' (Art. 26). Accordingly, the primary service of the EU and the CJEU is to help states resolve their collective action problems by preventing free riding in the form of protectionist policies that limit these four freedoms. Domestic bodies cannot be trusted to fit and 'weigh' the various objectives of the EU. But it is not obvious that EU bodies are always better qualified or positioned to 'balance' the various objectives of the EU (Kumm 2006: 522–524, Feichtner 2007, Howse and Nicolaïdis 2016: 265).

But states may have reasons to violate EU prohibitions against free riding. States may believe that human rights are at stake, or other bona fide values and objectives that are more important than the four freedoms. Disagreements about such 'balancing' of objectives occurred when the ECJ argued the primacy of EU law over fundamental rights secured in national constitutions (Internationale Handelsgesellschaft). The German Constitutional Court countered in several 'Solange' rulings that the ECJ must uphold minimum standards of protection of fundamental rights. And it would ultimately be for the German Constitution and its Court, rather than the ECJ, to identify those minimum standards (Internationale Handelsgesellschaft, Wünsche Handelsgesellschaft, Brunner).

Yet individual states cannot always be trusted to decide on whether and when any other objectives take priority over the four market freedoms, lest suspicions of abuse unravel general compliance. Subsidiarity arguments thus might support that some EU body determine whether a state complies and, if not, whether to permit it. On the other hand, these bodies may themselves have a centralizing institutional bias. The Protocol on Subsidiarity is supposed to counter this bias by spelling out the local units' authority to stop EU proposals.

The Protocol lays out two procedures for applying the TEU-conception of subsidiarity (Moens and Trone 2015). If one third of the national parliaments object to a draft proposal, they can trigger a control mechanism – the 'Yellow

Card procedure' (Art. 7, Cooper 2006, Resnik et al. 2008). Proposals concerning the area of freedom, security, and justice only require a threshold of one-quarter of the votes, arguably since these areas may be of greater concern for them. The European Commission or other drafters must decide whether to withdraw it or state its reasons to maintain or amend it. The CJEU adjudicates such cases (Art. 8). But just as central courts in many federations, the CJEU has a reputation for centralizing. Authors question its will and ability to be impartial (Bednar et al. 2001: 229, Shaw 2018).

The more serious 'Orange Card Procedure' does not involve the CJEU but only politically accountable bodies. If at least *half* of the national parliaments object, and the Commission maintains the proposal, it *must* be withdrawn if 55 per cent of members of the Council or 50 per cent of the members of European Parliament agree.

These complex procedures illustrate how the local units carefully allocate only the necessary authority to central bodies.

There have been very few cases where a party to a case for the CJEU has argued that there has been a substantive breach of the subsidiarity principle. Only one has been successful (Tobacco Advertising 2000; Kumm 2006). The Orange Card procedure has never been used, and the Yellow Card procedure has been used three times: regarding regulation of the right to strike – the Monti-II-Regulation (COM (2012) 130, Fabbrini and Granat 2013); whether to establish a European Public Prosecutor's Office (Fromage 2015); and changes to the cross-border posting of workers (Fromage and Kreilinger 2017). In the first case, the European Commission withdrew its proposal. In the other two, it refused. The Commission's response in the first case was criticized for offering no justification for its proposal, ignoring the requirement to show that a proposed action can only be achieved sufficiently at the EU level (Fabbrini and Granat 2013: 130–131). This underscores the importance of the authority to apply the principle of subsidiarity itself to contested matters. We consider another example concerning the topic of strikes in Section 8.

What are we to make of the low number of the various subsidiarity cases?[12] Some observe that the judicial review by the CJEU has been ineffective, because the Court tends to perform a cursory and weak review (Moens and Trone 2015). They instead suggest that the political review involving national parliaments may be more effective. However, critics hold that those mechanisms also serve next to no practical purpose. However, that conclusion is too hasty.

Firstly, the low number may show that the EU bodies generally 'get subsidiarity right'. Secondly, even though the Yellow and Orange Card procedures

[12] I am grateful to an anonymous reviewer who suggested to consider this issue in more depth.

have seldom been used, they may still have substantial 'shadow effects'. The prospects of these combinations of *political* and *judicial* review may cause the Commission to shape policy proposals in ways that avoid or pre-empt such reviews, to avoid embarrassment or even rejection of their plans. This is a complex mode of judicialization of politics (Alter et al. 2019, Pavone and Stiansen 2022). Among these shadow effects may be the Commission's efforts to specify the role of subsidiarity, including the use of a Regulatory Scrutiny Board that may in turn diffuse criticism from national parliaments (European Commission 2018: 4, European Commission 2024).

Thirdly, on the other hand, the few Yellow Card cases may reflect that national parliaments realize that the ultimate arbiter – the CJEU – has an institutional bias in favour of centralization, so that their attempts to block policy proposals by these mechanisms are likely to be futile. This explanation would not cover the lack of Orange Card cases, where the CJEU plays no role.

Fourthly, the practice of the Card procedures is arguably very limited. The Yellow Card procedure only requires that draft legislative acts indicate how 'any burdens, whether financial or administrative' falling upon various parties be minimized (Art. 5). Other burdens for other stated EU objectives need not be specified, so any such trade-offs among the many other objectives are ignored.

Finally, some hold that the CJEU is the proper institution to monitor subsidiarity because it is independent from all other institutions (Biondi 2012: 227). However, it also matters that the CJEU is not regarded as impartial concerning centralization. That may support reforms of the Yellow Card mechanism to reduce or remove the role of the CJEU. This would be in accordance with Theodor Schilling's prescient observation that several theories of subsidiarity may prohibit EU courts from having the last word regarding matters of subsidiarity (Schilling 1995: 4, cf. Cahill 2017: 218).

What are the characteristics of subsidiarity in the Preamble, Art. 5, the Protocol of the Lisbon Treaty, and in the Charter? They are arguably person-promoting conceptions rather than immunity-protecting, where central bodies exercise extensive authority to specify the objectives and to apply subsidiarity.

These conceptions of subsidiarity might appear to be immunity-protecting since they do not assess the quality of local units. However, the scope conditions for the principle limit it to EU member states who must ratify the ECHR and the Charter. Member states also allow further international scrutiny and criticism, including monitoring for suspected human rights violations or a risk of serious breaches of the values in Article 7 within Member States. Measures include dialogue, recommendations, and possible suspension of some of the rights of the Member State, including voting rights – but no procedure to exclude a State from the EU.

This scope condition arguably renders Lisbon subsidiarity more person-promoting. Other factors include states' limited veto within the EU due to high thresholds to initiate the Card procedures. Central bodies may override local units for the sake of the objectives of the social order and the contested primacy of market freedoms. The Orange Card Procedure appears to be the only exception to such central control.

Another element of Lisbon subsidiarity that renders it more person-promoting is that it and the Charter Preamble do not stop at the level of the state but mention regions and local bodies. This was partly due to the federal Member States Germany, Austria, and Belgium when negotiating the Amsterdam treaty. They insisted that

> action by the European Community in accordance with the principle of subsidiarity not only concerns the Member States but also their entities to the extent that they have their own law-making powers conferred on them under national constitutional law. (Germany Austria and Belgium 1997: 143)

Further evidence is the Yellow Card procedure which acknowledges that 'It will be for each national Parliament or each chamber of a national Parliament to consult, where appropriate, *regional parliaments with legislative powers*' (Art. 6). And the rules of procedure of the Committee of the Regions allow it to propose action against infringement of the subsidiarity principle (Committee of the Regions 2021: Rule 57).

To conclude, subsidiarity in the EU treaties can contribute to inter-systemic coherence. It appears that these conceptions may be understood as person-promoting rather than immunity-protecting. This may be relevant if conceptions of subsidiarity in the EU are considered as a source of subsidiarity as a general principle of law.

9 Intra-systemic Coherence and Subsidiarity: Human Rights in Europe

A principle of subsidiarity, however well justified, is of limited value on its own to alleviate the fragmentation of international law. To understand why subsidiarity contributes little to such intra-systemic coherence we consider a *hypothetical* tension between the two European legal orders, of the ECHR and the EU. These legal orders and the roles of subsidiarity within them differ in important ways (Cherubini 2015, Lock 2015: 167–242, Rosas 2022). Still, Sections 7 and 8 argued that subsidiarity arguments may justify the authority of both. Their jurisdictions overlap, and both include human rights among their objectives. Indeed, the term 'subsidiarity' appears in the treaties of both. The CJEU even claims to apply the same methodology as the ECtHR.

However, they may come to offer conflicting interpretations and judgements when seeking to accommodate both sets of legal norms. This underscores the importance of 'who has the authority to make a determination on a particular question arising under international law? And if more than one body has such authority, whose determination should prevail?' (Broude and Shany 2008: 102). The only point in what follows is to show why appeals to subsidiarity alone cannot guide this choice, without claiming that this presents the current or likely future policies of these courts (for other limitations cf. Da Silva 2023). Similar conclusions would seem to follow for other cases of fragmentation, for instance, between the international trade regimes and human rights (Alston 2002, Petersmann 2002, Suttle 2018).

9.1 The Accession of the EU to the ECHR – Potential Tensions

No clear conflict between the CJEU's and the ECtHR's interpretations and adjudications of their legal norms has occurred yet. This may change if – or when – the EU accedes to the ECHR and becomes subject to scrutiny by the ECtHR. TEU Art. 6(2) requires this accession, and a second draft for accession is currently under discussion (46+1 2023).

What is at stake with the accession? Conflicts might seem unlikely, but so do any benefits. The Charter of Fundamental Rights already requires the CJEU to abide by ECHR standards and ECtHR jurisprudence (52.3). And the ECtHR's 'Bosphorus Doctrine' assumes that states comply with the ECHR when they implement EU legislation (*Bosphorus Airways v. Ireland*). Still, review of the EU's legislation by the ECtHR may be beneficial. It might enhance intra-systemic coherence by reducing the risk that the CJEU overlooks any violation of the ECHR by any EU body. And review by the ECtHR can provide assurance among domestic populations and judiciaries that this is the case. Furthermore, the Bosphorus Doctrine is conditional: The ECtHR reserves the authority to assess EU protection of fundamental rights 'as regards both the substantive guarantees offered and the mechanisms controlling their observance, in a manner which can be considered at least equivalent' to the ECHR and is not 'manifestly deficient' (155, 156). Accession explicitly authorizes this.

Some might still think that accession will not change the Bosphorus Doctrine since subsidiarity is mentioned in the Preamble and would appear to favour that doctrine. It simply grants the EU a 'margin of appreciation' on an equal footing with the contracting states (46+1 2023 Para 7). However, the Bosphorus Doctrine renders the EU more deferential to the EU than towards member states (Flynn 2019: 123). And recall that the subsidiarity argument that justifies the Margin of Appreciation only applies to some rights and holds mutatis mutandis only if the CJEU is better informed about the local culture and legislation, and/or if the EU 'balances' rights on the basis of careful democratic deliberation. These assumptions remain to be defended in the case of the EU (Sommardal 2024).

Some actors also expect tensions, witnessed by reactions to the 2013 Draft Accession Treaty (47+1 2013). The CJEU argued in that this draft was incompatible with the EU treaties (Opinion 2/13, CJEU 2014, De Witte and Šejla 2015, Halberstam 2015, Isiksel 2016b). The revised draft released in 2023 sought to alleviate some of the problems (46+1 2023). Of main interest here is that the CJEU warned that the ECtHR would curb the CJEU's autonomy, since the ECtHR's interpretation of the ECHR would be decisive (CJEU 2014 para 36: 183–184). President of the ECtHR Dean Spielmann agreed that tensions might emerge. He warned against the CJEU's Opinion, that citizens will be victims if they are not be protected from EU human rights violations by external scrutiny (ECtHR 2015: 6).

Might subsidiarity arguments shed light on how to best 'harmonize' the relation between the EU and the ECHR to reduce such intra-systemic tensions? The following hypothetical example shows why that is unlikely. The treaties have different objectives that affect their courts' interpretations of human rights, their weight and scope. Appeals to subsidiarity alone offer little guidance about how to order these ultimate treaty objectives in order to resolve any tensions.

9.2 Example: Collective Action versus Freedom of Movement

A hypothetical example of the limited contribution of subsidiarity for inter-systemic coherence draws on the ECtHR's Holship case (Holship 2021a, Ellingsen 2022, Graver 2022). This topic has also been the subject of an Advisory Opinion by the EFTA Court, which interprets the European Economic Area (EEA) Agreement among Iceland, Lichtenstein, Norway, the EU, and the EU member states. EEA law is usually identical to EU law, so for our purposes this case illustrates the relevant tension (EFTA Court 2024.

A trade union has a collective agreement to load and unload all ships at a port. A shipping company planned to use non-unionized workers but would face a boycott by the union. This restricts the company's freedom of cross-border movement of goods. How *might* the ECtHR and the CJEU address this dilemma between the human or fundamental rights of trade unions (ECHR Art. 11, Charter Art. 12) and the EU's four fundamental freedoms – movement of people, goods, services, and capital? How, if at all, might subsidiarity arguments alleviate any disagreement?

Recall that subsidiarity arguments justify both of the international courts' authorities over states' policies for the sake of human rights and free trade. But the two courts perceive the tension differently. How will the CJEU 'balance' the market freedoms against human rights? The German Advocate General at the CJEU Juliane Kokkot – and the scholars Sabel and Gerstenberg – maintained that 'fundamental freedoms and fundamental Community rights are at the same level and must be harmonised' (Kokkott 2009: 171, Sabel and Gerstenberg 2010: 534–538, Isiksel 2016a).

When the CJEU reconciles these freedoms and rights, it has often prioritized economic freedoms over the human rights of collective labour rights (*Schmidberger, Laval, Viking, Omega*, Rebhahn 2009: 158, de Vries 2013a). For our purposes we can leave aside whether the CJEU is likely to alter this priority due to several changes: The Charter is now in effect. One Yellow Card case challenged the Commission' attempt to regulate collective action (Fabbrini and Granat 2013). Recent human rights violations in some member states may change the CJEU's perspectives. In any case, note that any such changes are at the discretion of the CJEU. This authority is at stake if the CJEU is reviewed by the ECtHR.

For the ECtHR the hypothetical case requires a very different balancing. It sees a conflict between the ECHR right to collective action against a market freedom which is not an ECHR right. It is possibly a public interest that might at most warrant a restriction of the freedom of association (ECHR Art 11.2).

Consider how these two courts might assess whether states are allowed to restrict the right to collective action for the sake of market freedom. They both allow some such restrictions, but only insofar as they impose minimal limitations on certain rights. The two courts prioritize different rights in this way.

The EFTA Court notes that 'The protection of workers has . . . been recognised as an overriding reason of general interest that may justify restrictions on the freedom of establishment' (EFTA Holship 2016). Consider what sorts of restrictions may be justified. If the CJEU follows its practice from the *Viking* case, it will regard the right to strike as *only* an instrument for worker protection, *only* to be permitted if *no other means are available* that restricts market freedoms less, and *only as a last resort* (*Viking*, de Vries 2013a). So: the more effectively the strike restricts the employer's free movement rights, the more difficult it is to justify the strike. In the extreme, there may be no case 'in which industrial action might be allowed to prevail over free movement rights' (Davies 2008: 143). Note that the point here is not to argue whether the CJEU is likely to continue this practice, but only to identify the sorts of tensions or conflicts that may arise among courts.

Compare this to the ECtHR which gives priority to the ECHR human right to strike (ECHR Art. 11.1). This right is the primary objective to be protected, and *restrictions* are *only permitted* when

> necessary in a democratic society in the interests of national security or public safety, for the prevention of disorder or crime, for the protection of health or morals or for the protection of the rights and freedoms of others. (Art. 11.2 ECHR, cf. UNISON v. United Kingdom)

The ECtHR does not require trade unions or workers to exhaust other alternatives before engaging in collective action. The difference is visible in the ECtHR's *Holship* judgement. To be effective, legitimate collective action may *have* to infringe on market freedoms – contrary to the CJEU's view, that any such infringements must be minimized. The ECtHR even underscored its potential disagreement with the CJEU's 'balancing' among rights in its earlier cases *Viking* and *Laval*. That, wrote the ECtHR, would only be appropriate if *both* rights were ECHR rights (para 118). But freedom of establishment – a market freedom – is *not* a human right.

9.3 Implications

For the CJEU, ECHR rights mainly appear as restrictions on market freedoms, and such restrictions must be minimized. For the ECtHR, market freedoms restrict ECHR rights, and these restrictions must be minimized (de Vries 2013b: 88). In short: The *objectives* of each court are *obstacles* in the eyes of the other.

This hypothetical example concerning the right to strike is meant to show the limited contribution of subsidiarity arguments to foster inter-systemic coherence. Subsidiarity arguments may justify both the CJEU and the ECtHR and how each of them balances rights but does not indicate whose balancing should be decisive in the choice between these two modes of harmonization (Cali 2007: 270). The result is that 'States that are signatories to the ECHR and are EU Member States [are left] between a rock and a hard place' (Barentsen 2023: 474). Subsidiarity would seem to offer little assistance, be it to the two international courts or to the domestic courts that must heed both of them. We need other arguments, for instance, about which treaty objectives should take priority in general or in particular cases.

The example also shows how and why dialogue among international judges may *not* provide the sort of intra-systemic harmonization we have reason to seek (Anderson 2005, Slaughter 2004, Young 2012). Systematic integration by means of treaty interpretation will not always be harmonious. Some such disagreements may be 'productive friction of "regime interaction" [that] may lead to a more responsive and effective international legal system than the sum of the constituent regimes' (Young 2012: 12). We should be wary of claims that legal norms, including fundamental rights and human rights, can or should simply be 'reconciled' with each other (Sabel and Gerstenberg 2010: 534). Reconciliation can yield different results, depending on who is entrusted with this authority. It remains to be seen whether such 'dialogues' are reliable paths of progress (Krisch 2010, Stone Sweet 2013) – or show how more powerful courts may do as they will, and the weaker do as they must. Those with a stronger self perception shared with important stakeholders may dominate (Fauchald and Nollkaemper 2012: 352, Shany 2012: 27–30).

Thus, we see that some of the CJEU's objections merit attention but can hardly be decisive. In particular, that the authority of the CJEU is challenged because it will be subject to review by the ECtHR is not an *objection*, but arguably part of the *objective* (Flynn 2019). A further implication may be that the presumption of the Bosphorus Doctrine may be triggered. The ECtHR has presumed that states' EU obligations comply with the ECHR. But its explicit statement about how *not* to 'balance' EU freedoms against ECHR rights may be a warning that the ECtHR will regard attempts by the CJEU to do otherwise as a 'manifest deficiency' of ECHR protection (Graver 2022). This is not an objection but a consequence.

This example also illustrates several scholars' warnings that common ground or overarching public values are contested (Alvarez 2016: 224, Carozza 2016: 55–59). Judges' important value-laden choices often go unnoticed, including the choices of objectives in their careful proportionality tests. These value choices may often reflect the particular service of their international court. The judges of a treaty body may understandably 'balance' in favour of their 'own' treaty's objectives (Koskenniemi 2012: 320; Shany 2012: 30): 'Where a court stands depends on where that court sits' (Keleman 2016: 117). One implication is that international judges, despite or even due to their professional training, often are not sufficiently impartial to decide among themselves which alternative intra-systemic 'balancing' should be decisive. To the contrary, they seem ill-positioned to render better decisions than the states, so they should not have the authority to do so.

A final observation is that subsidiarity may still give some guidance about who should choose among ways to increase intra-systemic coherence. There is no obvious reason to heed either of the contending court's claims to final authority over the other. The rebuttable preference for the local does not seem to be of help in selecting among them (Latimer 2018a: 302). Instead, substantive answers require substantive commitments to the priority of some objectives. A subsidiarity argument may still indicate which body should have this authority, rather than placing it with either international court. There are at least three other possibilities. The ICJ may take – or be granted – the authority to harmonize different sectors of international law (Andenas and Bjorge 2015). The International Labour Organization (ILO) already requested an advisory opinion from the ICJ on a related matter, concerning whether ILO Convention 87 includes a right to strike (ILO 2023). The ICJ might similarly be asked to address this issue. Several further alternatives give more local bodies that authority, in particular cases or generally when faced with such fragmentation. Individual domestic courts may decide which way to harmonize among the sectors of international law – at the risk of different resolutions in different jurisdictions, unless these courts coordinate among themselves. Or the decision may be placed with legislators or democratically accountable executives, nationally or at the European level, thus acknowledging the political nature of the choice. Other things equal, subsidiarity would support allocating this authority with legislators or accountable executives rather than independent judiciaries since the former are 'closer' to individuals.

This is what in fact happened: EU states decided the matter politically, by agreeing that the EU should become subject to the ECHR, and secure intra-systemic coherence accordingly. The states have decided that the CJEU must comply with the ECtHR's mode of harmonizing or incur legal responsibility for violations of the ECHR. The reactions of the CJEU to the latest draft accession agreement indicate that it may still take some time.

10 Conclusions

The presentations and reflections previously have addressed the grounds for various conceptions and theories of subsidiarity, and some implications for international law. The opacity of the discussions is reduced by some distinctions and elements: about which subject matters and units subsidiarity regulates; whether it concerns to establish, allocate, or use authority, including who is authorized to apply that principle itself; and the various objectives and standards of comparative efficiency it concerns. The many theories mustered in defence of various such conceptions of subsidiarity have all been found wanting. Before turning to some of subsidiarity's possible contributions to international law, consider how the aforementioned sketches allow responses to objections: that subsidiarity is an essentially contested apology for our Eurocentric global order in ways that threaten its legitimate contributions to international law and elsewhere; whether subsidiarity is anti-feminist, racist and imperialist, and too instrumental, justifying excessive state sovereignty and immunity for wicked governments, rather than robust responses to tragedies of human rights, climate change, and other global public bads.

10.1 Eurocentric?

Much research on the roots of subsidiarity identifies European and various Christian practices and theories. So subsidiarity seems vulnerable to ICJ judge Muhamed Bedjaoui's criticisms of classical international law: These are rules with a particular and problematic geographical and religious-ethical bias (Bedjaoui 1985, Anghie 2000).

Subsidiarity's European pedigree is undeniable: Subsidiarity in several European legal orders was clearly inspired by the German Constitution and by Catholic theory (Genesko 1986, Therborn 1989, Goldsmith 1996). Still, the traditions canvassed earlier alleviate but do not extinguish concerns that subsidiarity is unduly Eurocentric, at least in some senses. Section 2 noted some non-European, non Christian patterns, practices, and some principles of subsidiarity. And the premises of more plausible person-promoting theories are not exclusive to European political thought. Indeed, the Immunity and Non-domination versions with European pedigree seem less justifiable than person-promoting traditions that are also found outside Europe: of Confucius, Islam, and *Ubuntu*. As a concept subsidiarity might not be Eurocentric in problematic ways.

Some may object to the focus on the individual and their interests, and the assumption that the state should support them. This may appear incompatible with 'non-Western' philosophical traditions that prioritize social or political groups, or that grant states a different role. In response, some such claims by politicians are biased, possibly for political purposes. And to insist on distinct and unified Asian or African traditions opposed to 'the' European tradition ignores the diversity of cultures within and across geographical boundaries (Tang 1995, Sen 1997, Saul et al. 2011). Deplorable Western traditions dismiss the interests of many individuals well into the twenty-first century. And many non-Western normative traditions sketched earlier regard the individual as the ultimate unit of moral and political concern, insisting, as do many Western traditions, that individuals' interests include existing in society together with and for the sake of others, in different ways. Claims that responsible use of state power must be for the common good of present and future individual members of society are certainly part of the Western natural law tradition (Finnis 2011: 168, Follesdal 2022) but shared by versions of *Ubuntu*, Confucian, Hindu, and Islamic thought. Mencius (372–289 BC) specified the rulers' obligations on pain of tyrannicide (Gangjian and Gang 1995, Wood 1995: 170, Chan 1998). Islamic philosophers Ibn Abi-al-Rabi (ninth century), Al-Farabi and Ibn Khaldun (1332–1406) lay out how authorities must promote the common good (Ahmad 1965, An-Na'im 1990); as did Kautilya (c. 360–280 BC) in his treatise on good governance (Kautilya 2 BCE–3CE (1986), Hay 1988). Such scant references merely indicate shared values across 'civilizations' sufficient to question whether important disagreements merit the label 'Clash of Civilizations' (*pace* Huntington 1996). Criticisms and defences of various conceptions of subsidiarity cut across a 'West versus the rest' divide.

10.2 Too Instrumentalist?

Do subsidiarity arguments have an instrumentalist or functionalist bias, unable to neither offer a critical stance nor accommodate the intrinsic values of institutions? Many theories of subsidiarity sketched earlier criticize existing authorities and their powers; some justify abolishing empires or to create new authorities such as the EU or global governance for climate. Some subsidiarity arguments urge changes to existing bundles of authority such as marriage or the state.

Critics might fear that subsidiarity 'reduces the claim of rightful governance to a technocratic question of functional efficiency that will eventually undercut the nation-state's claims to loyalty' (Marquardt 1994: 617 in Barber 2005). Hooghe and Marks insist that functionalist explanations and justifications of authorities for collective benefits and coordination must be supplemented because authorities can also provide community, identity, and a sense of belonging. '[P]eople care about whether they have self-rule' – and 'about who exercises authority over them' (Hooghe and Marks 2009: 2, 2020: 218). In response several subsidiarity arguments – from Aristotle and *Ubuntu*, Wolff, Kant, and Raz – insist that persons and their interests are partly constituted by, and dependent on, their social and legal relations ranging from families to democratic citizenship. Some theories may allow or insist that subsidiarity arguments apply also to such intrinsic values.

10.3 Antifeminist, Racist, Imperialist?

Some theories of subsidiarity clearly have an anti-feminist, racist, and imperialist bias, including those of Immunity and Freedom. Some subsidiarity arguments supported the subjection of women in the form of gendered responsibilities in the family and the work place (Quadragesimo Anno, Pius XI 1931: 71), and even grant such 'domestic' matters immunity both from domestic public regulation and from international concern. And subsidiarity arguments may help explain the 'narrow and inadequate jurisprudence that has, among other things, legitimated the unequal position of women around the world rather than challenged it' (Charlesworth and Chinkin 2022: 1). Subsidiarity arguments have justified European states' imperialist colonization over 'less civilized' peoples elsewhere.

The sketches earlier diagnose the paths to such problematic conclusions and suggest revisions. Some crucial premises are false, as some authors such as Kant came to realize. Other unacceptable conclusions stem from contested objectives, be it specific ideals of human flourishing or a limited focus on protecting too few interests against too few risks. On the other hand, person-promoting conceptions of subsidiarity may structure and strengthen post-colonial and feminist critiques of the present international legal and political order. For instance, the current allocation of authority in international law seems flawed precisely because it fails to protect and promote the interests of the individuals subject to it. International law instead serves as an instrument of domination or unfair division of benefits and burdens. One of several debated topics is the distribution of veto power in the UN Security Council (Patrick 2023).

10.4 Subsidiarity and International Law

The arguments of this Element yield modest conclusions, also concerning subsidiarity and international law. Consider first the status of the state, and then the possible role of subsidiarity as a general principle of law.

One criticism against subsidiarity is that it takes for granted existing institutions such as sovereign states and their authority bundles – the present 'social ontology' (Brennan 2014). This inability to take a critical stance may be especially lamentable for TWAIL, for critical international legal theorists (Dunoff and Pollack 2022, Gathii 2022, Johns 2022), for feminist legal scholars, and for others wary of unacceptable biases in established practices and institutions, including in international law. Treaties embed power differentials – even about what counts as international crises that merit common concern among states – and how to decide any disagreements about this (Engle et al. 2022). Many see 'Westphalian' sovereignty as an 'increasingly dangerous vestige' that should be dismantled (Nordhaus 2006). Scholars warn about changes towards authoritarian international law, while the discussion of the ASEAN human rights regime (Ch 7.1) may support such objectives (Ginsburg and Huq 2018, Ginsburg 2020). State immunity prevents, rather than secures, the paramount 'global public good' of a response to climate change (Krisch 2014). Should we discard subsidiarity since it justifies this system of sovereign states and the international law they have established?

The overview confirms that some theories of subsidiarity are unduly immunity-preserving. They have justified, rather than criticized, existing unjust institutions. Yet the overview has also argued that more normatively justifiable subsidiarity arguments may favour new institutions and reform of existing ones – including the sovereign state and international law. Person-promoting theories of subsidiarity appear more normatively plausible and offer weaker support for a general presumption for the authority of the more local units. Their claims concern particular issue areas, and only under quite specific conditions.

The person-promoting conceptions do not dispute that states remain central in international law (Carozza 2016). But they challenge the normative justifiability of the current centrality of state consent in international law. So authors may be correct who claim, or warn, that subsidiarity *may* challenge the status of the state (Barber 2005, Davies 2006, Kumm 2006), and that 'subsidiarity … serves as a critical viewpoint with which to constantly undermine the internal and external foundations of … State Sovereignty' (Endo 2001: 36).

The more plausible person-promoting versions of subsidiarity canvassed earlier insist that, ultimately, the authority of states is justified only insofar as they and the web of institutions they are part of benefit individual persons' interests better than alternative institutional structures. So person-promoting subsidiarity would seem sceptical of the turn to authoritarian international law. They may support a more 'human-centred' trend in international law, such as the 'human-centric' treaties against slave trade and trafficking in persons, in favour of limits on war and workers' rights and other human rights (Gamble et al. 2005, Besson 2009, Nollkaemper 2010, Shaffer and Ginsburg 2012 : 12). Note that 'man-centric' may still unfortunately be more apt (Charlesworth et al. 1991, Charlesworth 1999: 386).

Person-promoting versions of subsidiarity appear to satisfy several conditions of general principles of law, one acknowledged source of international. Some conceptions describe many aspects of international law. And some such person-promoting conceptions also satisfy several conditions or criteria of general principles of law regarding their sources and contribution. We find patterns, practices, and principles of person-promoting subsidiarity in many national legal systems in different regions of the world beyond the West and Christianity, though many are arguably drawn from Western examples. Indeed, theories defending such conceptions seem less flawed than some other Western theories that favour immunity-preserving conceptions of subsidiarity. Person-promoting conceptions of subsidiarity also occur in international law, not only as description of some patterns but as practices and principles within the EU and the ECHR. It may thus be possible and appropriate to transpose a person-promoting conception of subsidiarity into the international legal system.

When it comes to its possible contributions to international law, a person-promoting conception of subsidiarity may promote cohesion or consistency and inter-systemic coherence, as general principles of law may also do. On the other hand, subsidiarity on its own is of limited value to further intra-systemic coherence: it does not alleviate the fragmentation of international law. It cannot serve as a 'meta-authority' to resolve conflicts among authorities

(Zürn 2018: 37) without some authoritative specification of the objectives of the political or legal order. In all these roles, subsidiarity must be supplemented by other principles lest it leaves open important choices about how to secure coherence. When such objectives are needed, conceptions of subsidiarity recommend that this is the task of authorities as close to the lives and interests of the individuals affected.

References

(Draft) Treaties, Protocols, Declarations

Statute of the International Court of Justice (ICJ) (1946). UN 33 UNTS 993.

ECHR, European Convention for the Protection of Human Rights and Fundamental Freedoms (1950). ETS 5; 213 UNTS 221.

Treaty Establishing the European Economic Community (EEC) (Treaty of Rome) (1957). 11957E/TXT.

ICCPR, International Covenant on Civil and Political Rights (1966a). GA Res. 2200 A (XXI) 999 UNTS 171.

ICESCR, International Covenant on Economic, Social and Cultural Rights (1966b). GA Res. 2200A (XXI).

Convention on the Law of Treaties (Vienna Convention) (1969a). 1155 UNTS 331.

Treaty of Southern African Development Community (SADC), Windhoek. (1992). www.sadc.int/documents-publications/show/865.

Protocol on the Application of the Principles of Subsidiarity and Proportionality (1997a). OJ C 115, 9 May 2008, 206–209.

Treaty on European Union (Amsterdam Treaty) (1997). OJ C340.

Statute of the International Criminal Court (ICC) (1998). 2187 UNTS 38544.

Treaty on European Union (Lisbon Treaty) (2007). OJ 2007/C 306/01.

Paris Agreement to the United Nations Framework Convention on Climate Change (2015). T.I.A.S. 16–1104.

Committee of the Regions. Rules of Procedure for the European Committee of the Regions (2021). OJ L 472/1.

46+1 Draft Revised Agreement on the Accession of the European Union to the Convention for the Protection of Human Rights and Fundamental Freedoms (2023). Council of Europe 46+1(2023)36.

47+1 Draft Agreement on the Accession of the European Union to the Convention for the Protection of Human Rights and Fundamental Freedoms (2013). 47 +1(2013)008rev2 (2013 DAA).

ASEAN Association of Southeast Asian Nations ASEAN Declaration [Bangkok Declaration] (1967). http://asean.org/the-asean-declaration-bangkok-declaration-bangkok-8-august-1967/.

ASEAN (2007). ASEAN Charter. www.aseansec.org/ASEAN-Charter.pdf.

ASEAN Human Rights Declaration (2012). www.asean.org/storage/images/ASEAN_RTK_2014/6_AHRD_Booklet.pdf.

Council of Europe Protocol No. 15 to the Convention on the Protection of Human Rights and Fundamental Freedoms (2013).

Copenhagen Declaration on the Reform of the European Convention on Human Rights System (2018). http://rm.coe.int/copenhagen-declaration/16807b915c.

European Parliament, et al. (2000). Charter of Fundamental Rights of the European Union. *OJ C 364/1–22*.

Cases and Opinions: CJEU – European Court of Justice /Court of Justice of the European Union

Stauder v. City of Ulm Sozialamt (1969b) 29/69 ECR 419.

Internationale Handelsgesellschaft (1970) ECR 1125.

Germany V Parliament and Council (Tobacco Advertising) (2000) C-376/98.

Schmidberger, Internationale Transporte und Planzüge v. Österreich (2003b) I-5659 ECR C-112/00.

Omega Spielhallen- und Automatenaufstellungs- Gmbh v. Oberbürgermeisterin Des Bundesstadt Bonn (2004) I-9609 ECR C-36/02.

International Transport Workers' Federation v. Viking (2007a) I-10779 ECR C-438/05.

Laval Un Partneri Ltd v. Svenska Byggnadsarbetareförbundet (2007b) I-11767 ECR Case C-341/05.

Opinion Pursuant to Article 218(11) TFEU (2014) 2/13 Curia.europa.eu.

Cases: ECtHR – European Court of Human Rights

The Cyprus Case, Greece V United Kingdom (1958) 176/1956 2 YB ECHR 174.

Belgian Linguistic Case (No. 2) (1968) 1 EHRR 252 Series A no 6.

Golder v. United Kingdom (1972) 1 EHRR 524.

Handyside v. United Kingdom (1976) 5493/72 24 (5493/72) 523.

Klass and Others v. Germany (1978) 5029/71 2 214.

Schenk v. Switzerland (1988) 10862/84.

Observer and Guardian v. United Kingdom (1991) 13585/88.

Z v. Finland (1997) 22009/93 25 EHRR 371.

Unison v. United Kingdom (2002) no. 53574/99.

Hatton v. United Kingdom (2003) 36022/97 611.

Bosphorus Airways v. Ireland (2005) 45036/98.

Kaya and Seyhan v. Turkey (2009) 30946/04.

Schalk and Kopf v. Austria (2010) 30141/04 53 EHRR 20.

Lindheim and Others v. Norway (2012) 13221/08 EHRR 985.

Holship, Norwegian Confederation of Trade Unions (LO) and Norwegian Transport Workers' Union (NTF) v. Norway (2021a) 45487/17.

Opinions: EFTA – European Free Trade Association

Holship Norge A/S Advisory Opinion (2016) EFTA Court E14/15 2016/C 73/06.

Cases: PCIJ – Permanent Court of International Justice

Advisory Opinion (1925). Interpretation of Article 3, Paragraph 2, of the Treaty of Lausanne. *PCIJ Series B Number 12,* 7.

Lotus (France v. Turkey) (1927) Ser A, No 10, 5, 18ff.

Cases: German Constitutional Court

Internationale Handelsgesellschaft v. Einfuhr und Vorratsstelle für Getreide und Futtermittel (Solange I) (1974) BVerfGE 37, 271.

Wünsche Handelsgesellschaft (Solange II) (1986) BVerfGE 73, 339.

Brunner v. European Union Treaty (Maastricht Urteil) (1993) BvR 2134/92 and 2959/92.

Other Sources

Acharya, A. & Stubbs, R. (eds.) (2008). *Theorizing Southeast Asian Relations*, London: Routledge.

Adler, M. (1990). The Exhaustion of the Local Remedies Rule after the ICJ Decision in ELSI. *International and Comparative Law Quarterly*, 39, 641–690.

Ahmad, I. (1965). *Sovereignty Islamic and Modern*, Karachi: Allies Book.

Alston, P. (2002). Resisting the Merger and Acquisition of Human Rights by Trade Law. *European Journal of International Law*, 13, 815–844.

Alter, K. (2008a). Agents or Trustees? *European Journal of International Relations*, 14, 33–64.

(2008b). Delegating to International Courts. *Law and Contemporary Problems*, 71, 37–76.

Alter, K., Hafner-Burton, E. M., & Helfer, L. (2019). Theorizing the Judicialization of International Relations. *International Studies Quarterly*, 63, 449–463.

Althusius, J. (1603 (1995)). *Politica Methodice Digesta*, transl. Carney, F.S. Indianapolis: Liberty Fund.

Alvarez, J. (2016). 'Beware: Boundary Crossings' – A Critical Appraisal of Public Law Approaches to International Investment Law. *Journal of World Investment and Trade*, 17, 171–228.

An-Na'im, A. (1990). Human Rights in the Muslim World. *Harvard Human Rights Journal*, 3, 13–52.

Andenas, M. (2015). Reassertion and Transformation. *Georgetown Journal of International Law*, 46, 685–734.

Andenas, M. & Bjorge, E. (eds.) (2015). *A Farewell to Fragmentation*, Cambridge: Cambridge University Press.

Andenas, M. & Chiussi, L. (2019). Cohesion, Convergence and Coherence of International Law. In Andenas, M., Fitzmaurice, M., Tanzi, A., & Wouters, J. (eds.), 9–34.

Andenas, M., Fitzmaurice, M., Tanzi, A., & Wouters, J. (eds.) (2019). *General Principles and the Coherence of International Law*, Leiden: Brill Nijhoff.

Anderson, K. (2005). Squaring the Circle? *Harvard Law Review*, 118, 1255–1312.

Anghie, A. (2000). What Is TWAIL: Comment. *Proceedings of the American Society of International Law*, 94, 39–40.

Aquinas, T. (1266(2002)). De Regno, Ad Regem Cypri. In Dyson, R. (ed.) *Aquinas*. Cambridge: Cambridge University Press, 5–51.

Arai-Takahashi, Y. (2001). *The Margin of Appreciation Doctrine and the Principle of Proportionality in the Jurisprudence of the ECHR*, Antwerpen: Intersentia.

(2013). The Margin of Appreciation Doctrine. In Follesdal, A., Peters, B., & Ulfstein, G. (eds.) *The European Court of Human Rights*. Cambridge: Cambridge University Press, 62–105.

Argentina, Brazil, Chile, Colombia, & Paraguay. (2019). Declaration to the Inter-American Commission on Human Rights, https://repositorio.uca.edu.ar/bitstream/123456789/8628/1/declaracion-sobre-sistema-interamericano.pdf.

Aristotle (1988). Politics. (Jowett, B. transl.) In Barnes, J. (ed.) *The Complete Works of Aristotle*. Princeton: Princeton University Press, 2, 1986–2129.

Aroney, N. (2007). Subsidiarity, Federalism and the Best Constitution. *Law and Philosophy*, 26, 161–228.

Bado, K. (2019). Good Governance as a Precondition for Subsidiarity. *Commonwealth & Comparative Politics*, 57, 242–259.

Bakunin, M. A. (1867(1972)). Federalism. In Avrich, P. & Dolgoff, S. (eds.) *Bakunin on Anarchy*. New York: Vintage Books. www.marxists.org/reference/archive/bakunin/works/various/reasons-of-state.html.

(1882(1970)). *God and the State*, Avrich, P. (ed.) New York: Dover.

(1971). *Bakunin on Anarchy*, Avrich, P. & Dolgoff, S. (eds.) New York: Vintage Books.

Ballara, A. (1998). *Iwi: The Dynamics of Māori Tribal Organisation from c. 1769 to c. 1945*, Wellington: Victoria University Press.

Barber, N. (2005). The Limited Modesty of Subsidiarity. *European Law Journal*, 11, 308–325.

(2018). Subsidiarity. In *The Principles of Constitutionalism*, Oxford: Oxford University Press, 187–218.

Barentsen, B. (2023). The Right to Collective Action. In Gerards, J. (ed.) *Fundamental Rights*. Cambridge: Cambridge University Press, 464–474.

Barroche, J. (2007). Subsidiarity and Jacques Delors. *Politique Europeénne*, 23, 153–177.

Barry, B. (1989). *Theories of Justice*, Berkeley, CA: University of California Press.

(1995). *Justice as Impartiality*, Oxford: Oxford University Press.

Baskwell, P. (2006). Kuyper and Apartheid. *HTS Theological Studies*, 62, 1269–1290.

Bates, E. (2016). Activism and Self-Restraint. *Human Rights Law Journal*, 36, 261–276.

Baumol, W. J. (1952). *Welfare Economics and the Theory of the State*, Cambridge, MA: Harvard University Press.

Beckman, R., Bernard, L., Phan, H. D., Hsien-Li, T., & Yusran, R. (2016). *Promoting Compliance*, Cambridge: Cambridge University Press.

Bedjaoui, M. (1985). Poverty of the International Order. In Falk, R., Kratochvil, F., & Mendelovitz, S. (eds.) *International Law*. Boulder: Westview, 152–154.

Bednar, J. (2008). *The Robust Federation - Principles of Design*, New York: Cambridge University Press.

Bednar, J. (2014). Subsidiarity and Robustness. *Nomos*, 55, 231–256.

Bednar, J., Eskridge, W. N., Jr., & Ferejohn, J. (2001). A Political Theory of Federalism. In Ferejohn, J., Rakove, J. N., & Riley, J. (eds.) *Constitutional Culture and Democratic Rule*. Cambridge: Cambridge University Press, 223–270.

Beer, S. (1986). Rule of the Wise and Holy. *Political Theory*, 14, 391–422.

(1993). *To Make a Nation*, Cambridge, MA: Harvard University Press.

Beitz, C. (2009). *The Idea of Human Rights*, Oxford: Oxford University Press.

Benedict XVI (2009). Caritas in Veritate. www.vatican.va/content/benedict-xvi/en/encyclicals/documents/hf_ben-xvi_enc_20090629_caritas-in-veritate.html.

Benvenisti, E. (1999). Margin of Appreciation, Consensus, and Universal Standards. *International Law and Politics*, 31, 843–854.

Berdan, F. (2017). Structure of the Triple Alliance Empire. In Nichols, D. & Rodriguez-Alegria, E. (eds.) *The Oxford Handbook of the Aztecs*. Oxford: Oxford University Press, 439–450.

Bergsmo, M. & Webb, P. (2010). International Criminal Courts and Tribunals, Complementarity and Jurisdiction. In Peters, A. & Wolfrum, R. (eds.) *Max Planck Encyclopedias of Public International Law*. Oxford University Press.

Berlin, I. (1958). *Two Concepts of Liberty*, Oxford: Oxford University Press.

Besson, S. (2009). The Authority of International Law. *Sidney Law Review*, 31, 343–380.

(2011). *Sovereignty*. In Peters, A. & Wolfrum, R. (eds.) *Max Planck Encyclopedias of Public International Law*. Oxford University Press.

(2016). Subsidiarity in International Human Rights Law. *American Journal of Jurisprudence*, 61, 69–107.

Bieber, R., Jacque, J.-P., & Weiler, J. H. H. (eds.) (1985). *An Ever Closer Union*, Luxembourg: European Communities.

Biondi, A. (2012). Subsidiarity in the Courtroom. In Biondi, A., Eeckhout, P., & Ripley, S. (eds.) *EU Law after Lisbon*. Oxford University Press, 213–227.

Blake, J. & Gilman, N. (2024). *Children of a Modest Star*, Palo Alto, CA: Stanford University Press.

Blecher, J. (2020). Scholars, Spice Traders, and Sultans. *Islamic Law and Society*, 27, 53–82.

Blichner, L. & Sangolt, L. (1994). The Concept of Subsidiarity and the Debate on European Cooperation. *Governance*, 7, 284–306.

Bogaards, M. (2023). Consociationalism and the State. *Nationalism and Ethnic Politics*, 1–19.

Bojun, Y. (ed.) (1980). *Mengzi* 孟子译著, Beijing: Zhonghua Shuju.

Bonner, M. (2005). Poverty and Economics in the Qur'an. *Journal of Interdisciplinary History*, 35, 391–406.

Borries, R. V. & Hauschild, M. (1999). Implementing the Subsidiarity Principle. *Columbia Journal of European Law*, 5, 369–388.

Brauch, J. A. (2005). The Margin of Appreciation and the Jurisprudence of the ECtHR. *Columbia Journal of European Law*, 11, 113–150.

Brauch, M. D. (2017). *Exhaustion of Local Remedies in International Investment Law*. IISD Best Practices Series. Winnipeg: International Institute for Sustainable Development.

Braybrooke, D. (1983). Can Democracy Be Combined with Federalism or with Liberalism? In Pennock, J. R. & Chapman, J. W. (eds.) *Liberal Democracy*. New York: New York University Press, 109–118.

Brems, E. (2019). Positive Subsidiarity and Its Implications for the Margin of Appreciation Doctrine. *Netherlands Quarterly of Human Rights*, 37, 210–227.

Brennan, P. (2014). Subsidiarity in the Tradition of Catholic Social Doctrine. In Zimmermann, A. & Evans, M. (eds.) *Global Perspectives on Subsidiarity*. Dordrecht: Springer, 29–48.

Broude, T. (2016). Selective Subsidiarity and Dialectic Deference in the World Trade Organization. *Law and Contemporary Problems,* 79(2), 53–74.

Broude, T. & Shany, Y. (eds.) (2008). *The Shifting Allocation of Authority in International Law*, London: Hart.

Brouillet, E. (2011). Canadian Federalism and the Principle of Subsidiarity. *The Supreme Court Law Review*, 54, 601–632.

Buchanan, A. (2003). The Making and Unmaking of Boundaries. In Buchanan, A. & Moore, M. (eds.) *States, Nations and Borders*. Cambridge: Cambridge University Press, 231–261.

Bull, H. (1977). *The Anarchical Society*, New York: Columbia University Press.

Burgess, M. (2000). *Federalism and European Union*, New York: Routledge.

Cahill, M. (2016). Sovereignty, Liberalism and the Intelligibility of Attraction to Subsidiarity. *The American Journal of Jurisprudence*, 61, 109–132.

(2017). Theorizing Subsidiarity. *International Journal of Constitutional Law*, 15, 201–224.

(2021). Subsidiarity as the Preference for Proximity. *American Journal of Jurisprudence*, 66, 129–143.

Cali, B. (2007). Balancing Human Rights. *Human Rights Quarterly*, 29, 251–270.

Carozza, P. (2003). Subsidiarity as a Structural Principle of International Human Rights Law. *American Journal of International Law*, 97, 38–79.

(2016). The Problematic Applicability of Subsidiarity to International Law and Institutions. *American Journal of Jurisprudence*, 61, 51–67.

Carter, W. M. (2008). Rethinking Subsidiarity in International Human Rights Adjudication. *Hamline Journal of Public Law and Policy*, 30, 319–333.

Cash, M. (2002). Distancing Kantian Ethics and Politics from Kant's Views on Women. *Minerva*, 6, 103–150.

Castellarin, E. (2019). General Principles of EU Law and General International Law. In Andenas, M., Fitzmaurice, M., Tanzi, A., & Wouters, J. (eds.) *General Principles and the Coherence of International Law*. Leiden: Brill, 131–148.

Cattaneo, C. & Bobbio, N. (1945(2010)). *Stati Uniti D'italia*, Roma: Donzelli.

Chan, J. (1998). A Confucian Perspective on Human Rights. In Bauer, J. R. & Bell, D. A. (eds.) *The East Asian Challenge for Human Rights*. New York: Cambridge University Press, 212–240.

(2003). Giving Priority to the Worst Off. In Bell, D. & Chaibong, H. (eds.) *Confucianism for the Modern World*. Cambridge: Cambridge University Press, 236–256.

(2012). Confucianism. In Palmer, M. & Burgess, S. (eds.) *The Wiley-Blackwell Companion to Religion and Social Justice*. Chichester: Wiley-Blackwell, 77–92.

(2014). *Confucian Perfectionism*, Princeton, NJ: Princeton University Press.

Chaplin, J. (2014). Subsidiarity and Social Pluralism. In Zimmermann, A. & Evans, M. (eds.) *Global Perspectives on Subsidiarity*. Dordrecht: Springer, 65–83.

Charlesworth, H. (1999). Feminist Methods in International Law. *The American Journal of International Law*, 93, 379–394.

Charlesworth, H. & Chinkin, C. (2022). *The Boundaries of International Law*, Manchester: Manchester University Press.

Charlesworth, H., Chinkin, C., & Wright, S. (1991). Feminist Approaches to International Law. *American Journal of International Law*, 85, 613–645.

Cherubini, F. (2015). The Relationship between the CJEU and the ECtHR in View of the Accession. *German Law Journal*, 16, 1375–1386.

Cohen, G. A. (1989). On the Currency of Egalitarian Justice. *Ethics*, 99, 906–944.

Colden, C. (1918–1937). *Letters and Papers*, New York: New York Historical Society Collections.

Confucius (200BC(1885)). *Book of Rites*, Oxford: Oxford University Press.

Cooper, I. (2006). The Watchdogs of Subsidiarity. *Journal of Common Market Studies*, 44, 281–304.

Cornell, D. (2012). A Call for a Nuanced Constitutional Jurisprudence. In Cornell, D. & Muvangua, N. (eds.) *Ubuntu and the Law*. New York: Fordham University Press, 324–332.

Couronne, V. & Maurel, R. (2019). Effective Domestic Remedy. In Peters, A. & Wolfrum, R. (eds.) *Max Planck Encyclopedias of International Law*. Oxford University Press.

Craig, P. (2012). Subsidiarity. *Journal of Common Market Studies*, 50, 72–87.

Crawford, J. (2012). Sovereignty as a Legal Value. In Crawford, J. & Koskenniemi, M. (eds.) *The Cambridge Companion to International Law*. Cambridge: Cambridge University Press, 117–134.

Crawford, J. (2014). *Chance, Order, Change: The Course of International Law, General Course on Public International Law*. Leiden: Brill.

Crema, L. (2010). Disappearance and New Sightings of Restrictive Interpretation(s). *The European Journal of International Law*, 21, 681–700.

Criddle, E. J. & Fox-Decent, E. (2016). *Fiduciaries of Humanity*, Oxford: Oxford University Press.

D'Aspremont, J. (2022). International Legal Positivism. In Dunoff, J. L. & Pollack, M. A. (eds.) *International Legal Theory*. Cambridge: Cambridge University Press, 63–81.

Da Silva, M. (2023). Subsidiarity and the Allocation of Governmental Powers. *Canadian Journal of Law & Jurisprudence*, 36, 83–111.

Dahl, R. A. & Tufte, E. (1973). *Size and Democracy*, Palo Alto, CA: Stanford University Press.

Dahl, R. A. (1970). *After the Revolution?* New Haven, CT: Yale University Press.

Dai, X. (2005). Why Comply? *International Organization*, 59, 363–398.

Dardanelli, P., Kincaid, J., Fenna, A., et al. (2018). Dynamic De/Centralization in Federations. *Publius: The Journal of Federalism*, 49, 194–219.

Davies, A. (2008). One Step Forward, Two Steps Back? *Industrial Law Journal*, 37, 126–148.

Davies, G. (2006). Subsidiarity. *Common Market Law Review*, 43, 63–84.

Davies, L. J. (2014). A Kantian Defense of the Right to Health Care. In Follesdal, A. & Maliks, R. (eds.) *Kantian Theory and Human Rights*. New York: Routledge, 70–88.

(2020). Kant on Welfare: Five Unsuccessful Defences. *Kantian Review*, 25, 1–25.

de-Shalit, A. (2018). *Cities and Immigration*, Oxford: Oxford University Press.

De Búrca, G. (1999). Reappraising Subsidiarity's Significance after Amsterdam. *Jean Monnet Working Paper 7/99*, New York University Law School. http://centers.law.nyu.edu/jeanmonnet/papers/99/990701.html.

de Klerk, W. A. (1975). *The Puritans in Africa*, London: R. Collins/Penguin.

De Schutter, H. (2019). Territoriality and Personality. In Lever, A. & Poama, A. (eds.) *Routledge Handbook of Ethics and Public Policy*. New York: Routledge, 129–142.

de Tocqueville, A. (1835(1969)). *Democracy in America*, New York: Anchor Books.

de Visser, J. (2010). Institutional Subsidiarity in the South African Constitution. *Stellenbosch Law Review*, 21, 90–115.

de Vries, S. (2013a). Balancing Fundamental Rights with Economic Freedoms according to the ECJ. *Utrecht Law Review*, 9, 169–192.

(2013b). The Protection of Fundamental Rights within Europe's Internal Market. In de Vries, S., Bernitz, U., & Weatherill, S. (eds.) *The Protection of Fundamental Rights in the EU after Lisbon*. Oxford: Hart, 59–94.

De Witte, B. & Šejla, I. (2015). Opinion 2/13 on Accession to the ECHR. *European Law Review*, 40, 683–705.

Del Moral, I. (2006). The Increasingly Marginal Appreciation of the Margin-of-Appreciation Doctrine. *German Law Journal*, 7, 611–623.

Delcamp, A., Balducci, M., & Busch, J.-D., et al. (1994). *Definition and Limits of the Principle of Subsidiarity*. Council of Europe.

Delors, J. (1989). Speech at the Opening Session. *EC Commission Document*, Speech/89/73.

Donnelly, J. (2003). *Universal Human Rights in Theory & Practice*, Ithaca, NY: Cornell University Press.

Dunoff, J. & Pollack, M. (eds.) (2022). *International Legal Theories*, Cambridge: Cambridge University Press.

Durieux, H. (2012). Subsidiarity, Anarchism, and the Governance of Complexity. In Loisen, J. & De Ville, F. (eds.) *Subsidiarity and Multi-Level Governance.* Wetteren: Universa, 15–26.

Duxbury, A. & Tan, H.-L. (2019). *Can ASEAN Take Human Rights Seriously?* Cambridge: Cambridge University Press.

Dyzenhaus, D. (2010). *Hard Cases in Wicked Legal Systems*, Oxford: Oxford University Press.

ECtHR – European Court of Human Rights. (2015). Annual Report 2014. www.echr.coe.int/documents/d/echr/annual_report_2014_eng.

EFTA Court – European Free Trade Association Court (2024). Jurisdiction – Organization. *https://eftacourt.int/the-court/questions-and-answers/.*

Ellingsen, H. (2022). Reconciling Fundamental Social Rights and Economic Freedoms: The ECtHR's Ruling in LO and NTF v. Norway (the Holship Case). *Common Market Law Review*, 583–604.

Elster, J. (2000). *Ulysses Unbound*, New York: Cambridge University Press.

Endo, K. (1994). The Principle of Subsidiarity. *Hokkaido Law Review*, 44, 2064–1965.

(2001). Subsidiarity and Its Enemies. *Robert Schuman Working Paper 24* [Online]. http://hdl.handle.net/1814/1733.

Engle, K., Nesiah, V., & Otto, D. (2022). Feminist Approaches to International Law. In Dunoff, J. & Pollack, M. (eds.) *International Legal Theory: Foundations and Frontiers*. Cambridge: Cambridge University Press, 174–196.

Espejo, P. O. (2012). Paradoxes of Popular Sovereignty. *Journal of Politics*, 74, 1053–1065.

European Commission (1975). Report on European Union. *Bull. EC Supp 5/75, COM (75) 400 Final.*

(2018). The Principles of Subsidiarity and Proportionality. *COM(2018) 703 Final.*

(2024). Regulatory Scrutiny Board. https://commission.europa.eu/law/law-making-process/regulatory-scrutiny-board_en.

Evans, M. (2014). Federalism and the Principle of Subsidiarity. In Zimmermann & Evans (eds.) *Global Perspectives on Subsidiarity*. Dordrecht: Springer, 201–226.

Eze, E. C. (1998). Modern Western Philosophy and African Colonialism. In Eze, E. C. (ed.) *African Philosophy: An Anthology*. Oxford: Blackwell, 213–221.

Eze, M. O. (2008). What Is African Communitarianism? *South African Journal of Philosophy*, 27, 106–119.

Fabbrini, F. (2018). The Principle of Subsidiarity. In Tridimas, T. & Schutze, R. (eds.) *Oxford Principles of EU Law*. Oxford: Oxford University Press, 221–242.

Fabbrini, F. & Granat, K. (2013). Yellow Card, but No Foul. *Common Market Law Review*, 50, 115–143.

Fauchald, O. K. & Nollkaemper, A. (eds.) (2012). *The Practice of International and National Courts and the (de)Fragmentation of International Law*, Oxford: Hart.

Feichtner, I. (2007). Subsidiarity. In Peters, A. & Wolfrum, R. (eds.) *Max Planck Encyclopedias of International Law*. Oxford University Press.

Fenton, W. N. (1998). *The Great Law and the Longhouse*, Norman, OK: University of Oklahoma Press.

Finnis, J. (2011). *Natural Law and Natural Rights*, Oxford: Oxford University Press.

(2016). Subsidiarity's Roots and History. *American Journal of Jurisprudence*, 61, 133–141.

Fishkin, J. (1986). Theories of Justice and International Relations. In Ellis, A. (ed.) *Ethics and International Relations*. Manchester: Manchester University Press, 1–11.

Flikschuh, K. (2010). Kant's Sovereignty Dilemma. *Journal of Political Philosophy*, 18, 469–493.

Flikschuh, K. & Ypi, L. (eds.) (2014). *Kant and Colonialism*, Oxford: Oxford University Press.

Flynn, T. (2019). *The Triangular Constitution*, Oxford: Hart.

Follesdal, A. (1998). Subsidiarity. *Journal of Political Philosophy*, 6, 190–218.

(2017). Exporting the Margin of Appreciation. *International Journal of Constitutional Law*, 15, 359–371.

(2021). Pure Public Goods and Beyond. In Zyberi, G. (ed.) *Protecting Community Interests through International Law*. Cambridge, MA: Intersentia, 59–98.

(2022). Current Contributions of the Natural Law Tradition to International Law. In Dunoff, J. & Pollack, M. (eds.) *International Legal Theories: Foundations and Frontiers*. Cambridge: Cambridge University Press, 39–62.

Follesdal, A. & Hix, S. (2006). Why There Is a Democratic Deficit in the EU. *Journal of Common Market Studies*, 44, 533–562.

Follesdal, A. & Muniz-Fraticelli, V. (2015). The Principle of Subsidiarity as a Constitutional Principle in the EU and Canada. *Les Ateliers de l'Éthique/The Ethics Forum*, 10, 89–106.

Franceschet, A. (2010). Kant, International Law, and the Problem of Humanitarian Intervention. *Journal of International Political Theory*, 6, 1–22.

Franklin, B. (1904). *Works*, New York: Putnam.

Fromage, D. (2015). The Second Yellow Card on the EPPO Proposal. *Yearbook of European Law*, 35, 5–27.

Fromage, D. & Kreilinger, V. (2017). National Parliaments' Third Yellow Card and the Struggle over the Revision of the Posted Workers Directive. *European Journal of Legal Studies*, 10, 125–160.

Gallie, W. (1956). Essentially Contested Concepts. *Proceedings of the Aristotelian Society*, 56, 167–193.

Gamble, J. K., Ku, C., & Strayer, C. (2005). Human-Centric International Law. *Tulane Journal of International and Comparative Law*, 14, 61–80.

Gangjian, D. & Gang, S. (1995). Relating Human Rights to Chinese Culture. In Davis, M. C. (ed.) *Human Rights and Chinese Values*. Oxford: Oxford University Press, 35–56.

Gathii, J. T. (2011). TWAIL: A Brief History of Its Origins, Its Decentralized Network, and a Tentative Bibliography. *Trade, Law and Development*, 3, 26–64.

(2022). The Agenda of Third World Approaches to International Law (TWAIL). In Dunoff, J. & Pollack, M. (eds.) *International Legal Theory: Foundations and Frontiers*. Cambridge: Cambridge University Press, 153–173.

Genesko, J. (1986). Der Wechselnde Einfluss Des Subsidiaritätsprinzip. In *Jahrbuch für Nationalökonomie und Statistik*. Stuttgart: Fischer, 404–421.

Germany, Austria, & Belgium (1997). Declaration on Subsidiarity Regarding the Treaty of Amsterdam, 143.

Ginsburg, T. (2020). Authoritarian International Law. *American Journal of International Law*, 114, 221–260.

Ginsburg, T. & Huq, A. (2018). *How to Save a Constitutional Democracy*, Chicago, IL: University of Chicago Press.

Goh, G. (2003). The 'ASEAN Way'. *Stanford Journal of East Asian Affairs*, 3, 113–118.

Goldsmith, M. (1996). Normative Theories of Local Government. In King, D. & Stoker, G. (eds.) *Rethinking Local Democracy*. London: Macmillan, 174–192.

Golemboski, D. (2015). Federalism and the Catholic Principle of Subsidiarity. *Publius*, 45, 526–551.

Golub, J. (1996). Sovereignty and Subsidiarity in EU Environmental Policy. *Political Studies*, 44, 686–704.

Goodin, R. (1992). *Green Political Theory*, Cambridge, MA: Polity/Blackwell.

(1996). Institutionalizing the Public Interest. *American Political Science Review*, 90, 331–343.

Goodin, R. E. (2007). Enfranchising All Affected Interests, and Its Alternatives. *Philosophy & Public Affairs*, 35, 40–68.

Goodman, R. & Peng, I. (1996). The East Asian Welfare States. In Esping-Andersen, G. (ed.) *Welfare States in Transition*. London: Sage, 192–224.

Gosepath, S. (2005). The Principle of Subsidiarity. In Follesdal, A. & Pogge, T. (eds.) *Real World Justice*. Dordrecht: Springer Netherlands, 157–170.

Graver, H. P. (2022). The Holship Ruling of the ECtHR and the Protection of Fundamental Rights in Europe. *ERA Forum*, 23(1), 19–32. https://doi.org/10.1007/s12027-022-00701-0.

Grimm, D. (2007). Proportionality in Canadian and German Constitutional Jurisprudence. *The University of Toronto Law Journal*, 57, 383–397.

Gussen, B. F. (2014). Subsidiarity as a Constitutional Principle in New Zealand. *New Zealand Journal of Public and International Law*, 12, 123–144.

Gädeke, D. (2009). Ubuntu and Neo-Republicanism. In Hull, G. (ed.) *Debating African Philosophy*. Abingdon: Routledge, 269–287.

Habermas, J. (1996). *Between Facts and Norms*, Cambridge, MA: MIT Press.

(2006). *The Divided West*, Cambridge: Polity Press.

(2012). *The Crisis of the European Union*, Cambridge: Polity Press.

Halberstam, D. (2015). 'It's the Autonomy, Stupid!'. *German Law Journal*, 16, 105–146.

Hampton, J. (1993). Contract and Consent. In Goodin, R. E. & Pettit, P. (eds.) *A Companion to Contemporary Political Philosophy*. Oxford: Blackwell, 379–393.

Harrington, J. (1656(1992)). *The Commonwealth of Oceania*, Cambridge: Cambridge University Press.

Hart, H. L. A. (1994). *The Concept of Law, New Edition*, Oxford: Clarondon Press.

Hay, S. (ed.) (1988). *Sources of Indian Tradition*, New York: Columbia University Press.

Hayek, F. A. (1944(1976)). *The Road to Serfdom*, London: Routledge & Kegan Paul.

Held, D. (2004). Democratic Accountability and Political Effectiveness from a Cosmopolitan Perspective. *Government and Opposition*, 39, 364–391.

Herman, B. (1993). *The Practice of Moral Judgment*, Cambridge, MA: Harvard University Press.

Hershovitz, S. (2011). The Role of Authority. *Philosophers' Imprint*, 11, 1–19.

Hirschl, R. (2020). *City, State*, Oxford: Oxford University Press.

Hoetjes, B. (1993). The European Tradition of Federalism. In Burgess, M. & Gagnon, A. (eds.) *Comparative Federalism and Federation*. Hempstead: Harvester, 117–137.

Hooghe, L. & Marks, G. (2009). A Postfunctionalist Theory of European Integration. *British Journal of Political Science*, 39, 1–23.

(2020). A Postfunctionalist Theory of Multilevel Governance. *The British Journal of Politics and International Relations*, 22, 820–826.

Howse, R. & Nicolaïdis, K. (2003). Enhancing WTO Legitimacy: Constitutionalization or Global Subsidiarity? *Governance*, 16, 73–94.

(2016). Toward a Global Ethics of Trade Governance. *Law and Contemporary Problems*, 79, 259–283.

Huan-Chang, C. (1911). *The Economic Principles of Confucius and His School*, New York: Longmans, Green.

Hueglin, T. O. (1987). Democracy, Democracy, and Federalism. In Bakvis, H. & Chandler, W. M. (eds.) *Federalism and the Role of the State*. Toronto: Toronto University Press, 32–54.

(1999). *Early Modern Concepts for a Late Modern World*, Waterloo: Wilfrid Laurier University Press.

Humboldt, W. V. (1850(1993)). *The Limits of State Action* Burrow, J. W. (ed.) Indianapolis, IN: Liberty Fund.

Hunt, M., Singh, R., & Demetriou, M. (1999). Is There a Role for the 'Margin of Appreciation' in National Law after the Human Rights Act? *European Human Rights Law Review*, 1, 15–22.

Huntington, S. P. (1996). *The Clash of Civilizations and the Remaking of World Order*, New York: Simon and Shuster.

Haakonssen, K. (2012). Christian Wolff. In Fassbender, B. & Peters, A. (eds.) *The Oxford Handbook of the History of International Law*. Oxford: Oxford University Press, 1106–1109.

Haas, E. B. (1958). *The Uniting of Europe*, London: Stevens and Sons.

Iber, S. (2011). *The Principle of Subsidiarity in Catholic Social Thought: Implications for Social Justice and Civil Society in Nigeria*, New York: Peter Lang.

Ike, O. & Edozien, N. (2001). *Understanding Africa: Traditional Legal Reasoning, Jurisprudence & Justice in Igboland*, Enugu: CIDJAP.

ILC – International Law Commission (2019). General Principles of Law – First Report. *A/CN.4/732*.

(2022a). General Principles of Law – Second Report. *A/CN.4/971*.

(2022b). General Principles of Law – Third Report. *A/CN.4/753*.

(2023). General Principles of Law – Draft Conclusions. *A/CN.4/L.982, GE.23–09074*.

ILC – International Law Commission Study Group (2006). Fragmentation of International Law. *UN Doc. A/CN.4/L.702 (18 July 2006)*.

ILO – International Labour Organization (2023). Request for Advisory Opinion from the International Court of Justice on the Interpretation of ILO Convention No. 87 with Respect to the Right to Strike. International Court of Justice General List no 191. www.icj-cij.org/sites/default/files/case-related/191/191-20231110-req-01-00-en.pdf.

Isiksel, T. (2016a). Disentangling Fundamental Rights and Market Freedoms. In *Europe's Functional Constitution*. Oxford: Oxford University Press.

(2016b). European Exceptionalism and the EU's Accession to the ECHR. *European Journal of International Law*, 27, 565–589.

Jachtenfuchs, M. & Krisch, N. (2016). Subsidiarity in Global Governance. *Law and Contemporary Problems*, 79, 1–26.

Jennings, R. & Watts, A. (1992). *Oppenheim's International Law Vol 1 Parts 2–4*. Burnt Mill: Longman.

John XXIII. (1963). Pacem in Terris. *Www.Vatican.Va/Holy_Father/John_Xxiii/Encyclicals/Documents/Hf_J-Xxiii_Enc_11041963_Pacem_en.Html*.

Johns, F. E. (2022). Critical International Legal Theory. In Dunoff, J. & Pollack, M. (eds.) *International Legal Theory*. Cambridge: Cambridge University Press, 133–152.

Johnson, B. (2017). *Pueblos within Pueblos*, Boulder, CO: University Press of Colorado.

Kalkbrenner, H. (1972). Die Rechtliche Verbindlichkeit Des Subsidiaritätsprinzip. In Hablitzel, H. & Wollenschläger, M. (eds.) *Recht und Staat*. Berlin: Duncker & Humblot, 515–540.

Kammerhofer, J. (2023). Legal Positivism. In Peters, A. & Wolfrum, R. (eds.) *Max Planck Encyclopedias of International Law*. Oxford University Press.

Kant, I. (1775(2007)). Of the Different Races of Human Beings. In Louden, R. B. & Zöller, G. (eds.) *Anthropology, History, and Education*. Cambridge: Cambridge University Press, 82–97.

(1784(1996)). An Answer to the Question: What Is Enlightenment? In Kant 1996, 11–22.

(1785(2007)). Determination of the Concept of a Human Race. In Kant 2007 (ed.), 143–159.

(1795(1996)). Toward Perpetual Peace. In Gregor, M. (ed.) *Kant: Practical Philosophy*. Cambridge: Cambridge University Press, 311–352.

(1991). *Kant's Political Writings (2nd Ed.)*, Reiss, H. S. (ed.) Cambridge: Cambridge University Press.

(1996). *Practical Philosophy*, Gregor, M. (ed.) Cambridge: Cambridge University Press.

(2007). *Anthropology, History, and Education*, Louden, R. B. & Zöller, G. (eds.) Cambridge: Cambridge University Press.

Kapteyn, P. (1991). Community Law and the Principle of Subsidiarity. *Revue des Affaires Européennes*, 2, 35–43.

Kaufmann, F.-X. (1988). The Principle of Subsidiarity Viewed by the Sociology of Organizations. *The Jurist*, 48, 275–291.

Kautilya (2BCE-3CE (1986)). *Arthashastra*, Bombay: University of Bombay.

Keleman, R. D. (2016). The CJEU in the 21st Century. *Law and Contemporary Problems*, 79, 117–140.

King, L. & Blake, M. (2018). Global Cities, Global Justice? *Journal of Global Ethics*, 14, 332–352.

Kleingeld, P. (2014). Kant's Second Thoughts on Colonialism. In Flikschuh, K. & Ypi, L. (eds.) *Kant and Colonialism*. Oxford: Oxford University Press, 43–67.

Klumpp, M. (2013). *Schiedsgerichtsbarkeit und Ständiges Revisionsgericht Des Mercosur*, Berlin: Springer.

Kokkott, J. (2009). The ECJ's Interpretation of the Posting Directive in the Laval and Rüffert Judgements. In Scholz, O. & Ulrich Becker, U. (eds.) *Die Auswirkungen Der Rechtsprechung Des Europäischen Gerichtshofs Auf Das Arbeitsrecht Der Mitgliedstaaten*. Baden-Baden: Nomos, 165–172.

Kongshøj, K. (2015). *Social Citizenship in China and the Nordic Countries*, Aalborg: Aalborg University.

Koskenniemi, M. (2012). Hegemonic Regimes. In Young, M. A. (ed.) *Regime Interaction in International Law*. Cambridge: Cambridge University Press, 305–324.

Kratochvil, J. (2011). The Inflation of the Margin of Appreciation by the ECtHR. *Netherlands Quarterly of Human Rights*, 29, 324–357.

Krisch, N. (2010). *Beyond Constitutionalism*, Oxford: Oxford University Press.

(2014). The Decay of Consent. *American Journal of International Law*, 108, 1–40.

Kumm, M. (2006). Constitutionalising Subsidiarity in Integrated Markets. *European Law Journal*, 12, 503–533.

(2009). The Cosmopolitan Turn in Constitutionalism. In Dunoff, J. & Trachtman, J. (eds.) *Ruling the World?* Cambridge: Cambridge University Press, 257–324.

(2016). Sovereignty and the Right to Be Left Alone. *Law and Contemporary Problems*, 79, 239–258.

Kuyper, A. (1880). *Souvereiniteit in Eigen Kring*, Amsterdam: J. H. Kruyt.

(1898(2016)). *Het Calvinisme*, Australia: Leopold.

Kuyperus, T. (1999). *State, Civil Society and Apartheid in South Africa*, London: Palgrave.

Kymlicka, W. (1995). *Multicultural Citizenship*, Oxford: Oxford University Press.

Laffranque, J. (2015). Subsidiarity. *Seminar at Opening of Judicial Year, Strasbourg* [Online]. https://cutt.ly/gED4aBC.

Lamy, P. (2012). *Speech at the Singapore Global Dialogue: Governance of a Multipolar World Order* (21 September 2012) www.wto.org/english/news_e/sppl_e/sppl248_e.htm.

Larmore, C. (2001). A Critique of Philip Pettit's Republicanism. *Philosophical Issues*, 11, 229–243.

Latimer, T. (2018a). Against Subsidiarity. *Journal of Political Philosophy*, 26, 282–303.

(2018b). The Principle of Subsidiarity. *Constellations*, 25, 586–601.

Lecheler, H. (1993). *Das Subsidiaritätsprinzip*, Berlin: Duncker & Humblot.

Lemco, J. (1991). *Political Stability in Federal Governments*, New York: Praeger.

Leo XIII (1891(1981)). Rerum Novarum. *www.Vatican.Va/Holy_Father/Leo_Xiii/Encyclicals/Documents/Hf_L-Xiii_Enc_15051891_Rerum-Novarum_en.html*.

Lester, A. (2009). The ECtHR after 50 Years. *European Human Rights Law Review*, 4, 461–478.

Letsas, G. (2006). Two Concepts of the Margin of Appreciation. *Oxford Journal of Legal Studies*, 26, 705–732.

Levy, J. (2007). Self-Determination, Non-Domination, and Federalism. *Hypatia*, 23, 60–78.

Lijphart, A. (1968). *The Politics of Accommodation*, Berkeley, CA: University of California Press.

(1979). Consociation and Federation. *Canadian Journal of Political Science*, 22, 499–515.

(1995). Self-Determination Versus Pre-Determination of Ethnic Minorities in Power-Sharing Systems. In Kymlicka, W. (ed.) *The Rights of Minority Cultures*. Oxford: Oxford University Press, 275–288.

Lloyd, G. (1993). *Man of Reason*, London: Routledge.

Lloyd, P. (1971). The Political Development of Yoruba Kingdoms in the Eighteenth and Nineteenth Centuries. *Royal Anthropological Institute Occasional Paper*, 31.

Lock, T. (2015). *The European Court of Justice and International Courts*, Oxford: Oxford University Press.

Lockhart, J. (1992). *The Nahuas after the Conquest*, Palo Alto, CA: Stanford University Press.

Lööw, L. (2013). *The Principle of Subsidiarity*, Uppsala: Master's Thesis, Faculty of Law.

MacCormick, N. (1995). Sovereignty, Democracy and Subsidiarity. In Bellamy, R., Bufacchi, V., & Castiglione, D. (eds.) *Democracy and Constitutional Culture in the Union of Europe*. London: Lothian Foundation.

(1997). Democracy, Subsidiarity, and Citizenship in the 'European Commonwealth'. *Law and Philosophy*, 16, 331–356.

(1999). *Questioning Sovereignty: Law, State, and Nation in the European Commonwealth*, Oxford: Oxford University Press.

Macedo, S. (1993). Toleration and Fundamentalism. In Goodin, R. E. & Pettit, P. (eds.) *A Companion to Contemporary Political Philosophy*. Oxford: Blackwell, 622–628.

Mackenzie, S. (1991). Assessment and Introduction. In *Subsidiarity: The Challenge of Change. Proceedings of the Jacques Delors Colloquium 1991*. Maastricht: European Institute of Public Administration.

Macklem, P. (2006). Militant Democracy, Legal Pluralism, and the Paradox of Self-Determination. *International Journal of Constitutional Law*, 4, 488–516.

Madison, J. (1787(1961)). The Federalist No. 10. In Rossiter, C. (ed.) *Federalist Papers*, New York: Mentor.

(1787(1961)). The Federalist No. 20. In Rossiter, C. (ed.) *Federalist Papers*, New York: Mentor, 134–137.

(1788 (1961)). The Federalist No. 51. In Rossiter, C. (ed.) *Federalist Papers*, New York: Mentor.

Maliks, R. (2012). Kant and Cosmopolitanism. *Metaphilosophy*, 43, 714–718.

(2014). *Kant's Politics in Context*, Oxford: Oxford University Press.

Manning, J. (2011). Separation of Powers as Ordinary Interpretation. *Harvard Law Review*, 124.

Marquardt, P. (1994). Subsidiarity and Sovereignty in the European Union. *Fordham International Law Journal*, 18, 616–640.

Mbiti, J. S. (1969). *African Religions and Philosophy*, New Hampshire, NH: Heinemann.

Mencius (2003). *Mencius: A Bilingual Edition*, Hong Kong: Chinese University Press.

Mendus, S. (1992). Kant: "An Honest but Narrow-Minded Bourgeois"? In Williams, H. (ed.) *Essays on Kant's Political Philosophy*. Cardiff: University of Wales Press, 166–190.

Merkouris, P. (2017). In Dubio Mitius. In Klingler, J., Parkhomenko, Y., & Salonidis, C. (eds.) *Between the Lines of the Vienna Convention*. Alphen aan den Rijn: Kluwer, 259–306.

Metz, T. (2007). Toward an African Moral Theory. *Journal of Political Philosophy*, 15, 321–341.

(2011). Ubuntu as a Moral Theory and Human Rights in South Africa. *African Human Rights Law Journal*, 11, 532–559.

(2021). *A Relational Moral Theory: African Ethics in and Beyond the Continent*, Oxford: Oxford University Press.

Mikkola, M. (2011). Kant on Moral Agency and Women's Nature. *Kantian Review*, 16, 89–111.

Mill, J. S. (1873(1969)). *Autobiography*, Boston, MA: Houghton Mifflin.

Miller, D. (1995). *On Nationality*, Oxford: Oxford University Press.

Millon-Delsol, C. (1993). *Le Principe de Subsidiarité*, Paris: Presses Universitaires De France.

Moens, G. A. & Trone, J. (2015). The Principle of Subsidiarity in EU Judicial and Legislative Practice. *Journal of Legislation*, 41, 65–102.

Montesquieu, B. D. (1748(2002)). *Spirit of Laws*, Amherst, NY: Prometheus.

Moravcsik, A. (1995). Explaining International Human Rights Regimes. *European Journal of International Relations*, 1, 157–189.

Mosler, H. (1999). General Principles of Law. In *Encyclopedia of Public International Law*. Amsterdam: Elsevier, 511–526.

Mosser, K. (1999). Kant and Feminism. *Kant-studien*, 90, 322–353.

Mounier, E. (1957). *Le Personnalisme*, Paris: Presses Universitaires De France.

Musgrave, R. (1959). *The Theory of Public Finance*, New York: McGraw-Hill.

Möllers, C. (2011). Multi-Level Democracy. *Ratio Juris*, 24, 247–266.

Nagel, T. (1987). Moral Conflict and Political Legitimacy. *Philosophy and Public Policy*, 16, 215–240.

Neuman, G. (2013). Subsidiarity. In Shelton, D. (ed.) *Oxford Handbook of International Human Rights Law*. Oxford: Oxford University Press, 360–378.

Neunreither, K. (1993). Subsidiarity as a Guiding Principle for European Community Activities. *Government and Opposition*, 28, 206–220.

Nine, C. (2022). *Sharing Territories: Overlapping Self-Determination and Resource Rights*. Oxford: Oxford University Press.

Nollkaemper, A. (2010). Rethinking the Supremacy of International Law. *Zeitschrift für öffentliches Recht*, 65, 65–85.

Nordhaus, W. D. (2006). Paul Samuelson and Global Public Goods. In Szenberg, M., Ramrattan, L., & Gottesman, A. A. (eds.) *Samuelsonian Economics and the Twenty-First Century*. Oxford: Oxford University Press, 88–98.

Oates, W. (1972). *Fiscal Federalism*, New York: Harcourt Brace Jovanovich.

(2005). Toward a Second-Generation Theory of Fiscal Federalism. *International Tax and Public Finance*, 12, 349–373.

Okin, S. M. (1989). Reason and Feeling in Thinking about Justice. *Ethics*, 99, 229–249.

1979(2013). *Women in Western Political Thought*, Satz, D. (ed.) Princeton, NJ: Princeton University Press.

Olson, M. (1965). *The Logic of Collective Action*, Cambridge, MA: Harvard University Press.

Orakhelashvili, A. (2003). Restrictive Interpretation of Human Rights Treaties in the Recent Jurisprudence of the ECtHR. *European Journal of International Law*, 14, 529–568.

Otto, D. (2016). Feminist Approaches to International Law. In Orford, A. & Hoffmann, F. (eds.) *The Oxford Handbook of the Theory of International Law*. Oxford: Oxford University Press, 488–504.

Padou-Schioppa, T. (1995). Economic Federalism and the European Union. In Knop, K., Ostry, S., Simeon, R., & Swinton, K. (eds.) *Rethinking Federalism*. Vancouver: University of British Columbia Press, 154–165.

Pateman, C. (1988). *The Sexual Contract*, Stanford: Stanford University Press.

Patrick, S. (ed.) (2023). *UN Security Council Reform*. Washington, DC: Carnegie Endowment for International Peace.

Paulus, A. (2005). Jus Cogens in a Time of Hegemony and Fragmentation. *Nordic Journal of International Law*, 74, 297–334.

(2008). Subsidiarity, Fragmentation and Democracy. In Broude, T. & Shany, Y. (eds.) *The Shifting Allocation of Authority in International Law*. Oxford: Hart, 193–213.

(2013). Human Rights Protection in a European Network of Courts. *Proceedings of the American Society of International Law*, 107, 174–182.

Pavel, C. (2014). *Divided Sovereignty*, Oxford: Oxford University Press

Pavone, T. & Stiansen, Ø. (2022). The Shadow Effect of Courts. *American Political Science Review*, 116, 322–336.

Pellet, A. (2000). State Sovereignty and the Protection of Fundamental Human Rights. *Pugwash Occasional Papers*, 1, 37–45.

Peters, A. (2006). Compensatory Constitutionalism. *Leiden Journal of International Law*, 19, 579–610.

(2009). Humanity as the Alpha and Omega of Sovereignty. *European Journal of International Law*, 20, 513.

Peters, P. (1997). Exhaustion of Local Remedies. *Netherlands International Law Review*, 44, 233–243.

Petersmann, E.-U. (2002). Time for a United Nations 'Global Compact' for Integrating Human Rights into the Law of Worldwide Organizations. *European Journal of International Law*, 13, 621–650.

Pettit, P. (1997). *Republicanism*, Oxford: Clarendon Press.

Pius XI (1931). Quadragesimo Anno. *www.vatican.va/content/pius-xi/en/encyclicals/documents/hf_p-xi_enc_19310515_quadragesimo-anno.html.*

Pizano, P. (2020). *Chile: The Risk of a New Constitution.* McCain Institute. *www.mccaininstitute.org/resources/blog/chile-the-risks-of-a-new-constitution/.*

Pollack, M. (2002). The End of Creeping Competence? *Journal of Common Market Studies*, 38, 519–538.

Prichard, A. (2007). Justice, Order and Anarchy. *Millennium*, 35, 623–645.

(2022). *Anarchism*, Oxford: Oxford University Press.

Prodi, R. (2000). *Europe as I See It*, Cambridge, MA: Polity Press.

Proudhon, P.-J. (1863(1979)). *The Principle of Federation and the Need to Reconstitute the Party of the Revolution*, Toronto: Toronto University Press.

(1994). *What Is Property?* Cambridge: Cambridge University Press.

Qian, Y. & Weingast, B. (1997). Federalism as a Commitment to Preserving Market Incentives. *The Journal of Economic Perspectives*, 11, 83–92.

Ramose, M. (1999). *African Philosophy through Ubuntu*, Harare: Mond Books.

Rawls, J. (1971). *A Theory of Justice*, Cambridge, MA: Harvard University Press.

Raz, J. (1986). *The Morality of Freedom*, Oxford: Clarendon Press.

(2003). Numbers, with and without Contractualism. *Ratio*, 16, 346–367.

(2006). The Problem of Authority. *Minnesota Law Review*, 90, 1003–1044.

(2010). Human Rights in the Emerging World Order. *Transnational Legal Theory*, 1, 31–47.

(2013). On Waldron's Critique of Raz on Human Rights. *Oxford Legal Studies Research Paper No. 80/2013*, Oxford.

(2017). Why the State? In Roughan, N. & Halpin, A. (eds.) *In Pursuit of Pluralist Jurisprudence*. Cambridge: Cambridge University Press, 136–162.

(2019). The Future of State Sovereignty. In Sadurski, W., Sevel, M., & Walton, K. (eds.) *Legitimacy: The State and Beyond*. Oxford: Oxford University Press, 69–91.

Rebhahn, R. (2009). The Recent Jurisprudence of the ECJ. In Scholz, O. & Becker, U. (eds.) *Die Auswirkungen Der Rechtsprechung Des Europäischen Gerichtshofs*. Baden: Nomos, 157–163.

Reinicke, W. (1998). *Global Public Policy*, Washington, DC: Brookings.

Resnik, J., Civin, J., & Frueh, J. (2008). Ratifying Kyoto at the Local Level. *Arizona Law Review*, 50, 709–786.

Riker, W. H. (1964). *Federalism*, Boston, MA: Little, Brown.

Ripstein, A. (2009). *Force and Freedom*, Cambridge, MA: Harvard University Press.

(2014). Kant's Juridical Theory of Colonialism. In Flikschuh & Ypi (eds.), 145–169.

Rodden, J. A. (2006). *Hamilton's Paradox*, New York: Cambridge University Press.

Rosas, A. (2022). The CJEU. *Journal of Human Rights Practice*, 14, 204–214.

Sabel, C. & Gerstenberg, O. (2010). Constitutionalising an Overlapping Consensus. *European Law Journal*, 16, 511–550.

Samuelson, P. A. (1954). The Pure Theory of Public Expenditure. *Review of Economics and Statistics*, 36, 387–389.

(1955). Diagrammatic Exposition of Public Expenditure. *Review of Economics and Statistics*, 21, 350–356.

Saul, B., Mowbray, J., & Baghoomians, I. (2011). The Last Frontier of Human Rights Protection. *Australian International Law Journal*, 18, 23–52.

Scanlon, T. M. (1978). Rights, Goals and Fairness. In Hampshire, S. (ed.) *Public and Private Morality*. Cambridge: Cambridge University Press, 93–112.

(1982). Contractualism and Utilitarianism. In Sen, A. & Williams, B. (eds.) *Utilitarianism and Beyond*. Cambridge: Cambridge University Press, 103–128.

(1992). The Aims and Authority of Moral Theory. *Oxford Journal of Legal Studies*, 12(1), 1–23.

(1995). Moral Theory. *Philosophy and Phenomenological Research*, 55, 343–356.

Schachter, O. (1982). *General Course in Public International Law: Recueil Des Cours*, Leiden: Nijhoff.

Scharpf, F. (1988). The Joint Decision Trap. *Public Administration*, 66, 239–278.

Schilling, T. (1995). Subsidiarity as a Rule and a Principle, Or: Taking Subsidiarity Seriously. *Jean Monnet Working Papers* [Online]. https://jeanmonnetprogram.org/archive/papers/95/9510ind.html.

Schott, R. M. (ed.) (1997). *Feminist Interpretations of Immanuel Kant*, University Park, PA: Pennsylvania State University Press.

Schuman, R. (1950). Declaration of May 9. www.robert-schuman.org/anglais/robert-schuman/declaration.html.

Schumpeter, J. A. (1976). *Capitalism, Socialism and Democracy*, London: Allen and Unwin.

Schwarte, J. (1975). *Gustav Gundlach S.J. (1892–1963)*, Munich: Schoningh.

Sen, A. K. (1982). *Choice, Welfare and Measurement*, Cambridge, MA: MIT Press.

(1997). Human Rights and Asian Values. *The New Republic*, July 14, 33–40.

Shaffer, G. & Ginsburg, T. (2012). The Empirical Turn in International Legal Scholarship. *American Journal of International Law*, 106, 1–46.

Shany, Y. (2005). Toward a General Margin of Appreciation Doctrine? *European Journal of International Law*, 16, 907–940.

(2012). One Law to Rule Them All. In Fauchald, O. K. & Nollkaemper, A. (eds.) *The Practice of International and National Courts and the (de) Fragmentation of International Law*. Oxford: Hart, 15–34.

Shapiro, S. (2006). What Is the Internal Point of View. *Fordham Law Review*, 75, 1157–1170.

Shaw, K. (2018). *The CJEU: Subsidiarity and Proportionality*, Boston, MA: Brill – Nijhoff.

Simma, B. & Paulus, A. (1999). The Responsibility of Individuals for Human Rights Abuses in Internal Conflicts. *The American Journal of International Law*, 93, 302–316.

Shutte, A. (2001). *Ubuntu*, Cape Town: Cluster.

Skinner, Q. (1984). The Idea of Negative Liberty. In Rorty, R., Skinner, Q., & Schneewind, J. B. (eds.) *Philosophy in History*. Cambridge: Cambridge University Press, 204–219.

Slaughter, A.-M. (2000). A Liberal Theory of International Law. *Proceedings American Society of International Law*, 94, 240.

(2004). *A New World Order*, Princeton, NJ: Princeton University Press.

Smith, N. D. (1983). Plato and Aristotle on the Nature of Women. *Journal of the History of Philosophy*, 21, 467–478.

Sommardal, J. (2024). The ECHR and the EU Legal Order [Unpublished].

Spano, R. (2018). The Future of the ECtHR. *Human Rights Law Review*, 18, 473–493.

Spielmann, D. (2012). Allowing the Right Margin. *Cambridge Yearbook of European Legal Studies*, 14, 381–418.

Stone Sweet, A. (2013). The Structure of Constitutional Pluralism. *International Journal of Constitutional Law*, 11, 491–500.

Stone Sweet, A. & Andenas, M. (2022). The Law and Politics of the General Principles of Law in the Twenty-First Century. *University of Hong Kong Faculty of Law Research Paper No. 56*, University of Hong Kong, Faculty of Law.

Stone Sweet, A. & Ryan, C. (2021). *A Cosmopolitan Legal Order*, Oxford: Oxford University Press.

Stråth, B. (2023). *Ujamaa and Ubuntu*, London: Routledge.

Sun, X. (2020). Reestablishing the Significance of 'Family' in the Modern World. *Contemporary Social Sciences*, 4, 44–59.

Suttle, O. (2018). *Distributive Justice and World Trade Law*, Cambridge: Cambridge University Press.

Sweeney, J. (2005). Margins of Appreciation. *International and Comparative Law Quarterly*, 54, 459–474.

Tang, J. (ed.) (1995). *Human Rights and International Relations in the Asia-Pacific Region*, London: Pinter.

Therborn, G. (1989). 'Pillarization' and 'Popular Movements'. In Castles, F. G. (ed.) *The Comparative History of Public Policy*. Cambridge, MA: Polity Press, 192–241.

Tiebout, C. M. (1956). A Pure Theory of Local Expenditures. *Journal of Political Economy*, 64, 416–424.

Tindemans, L. (1976). European Union. *Bull. E.C. 5–1975 and Bull. E.C. 9–1975.*

TNI-Transnational Institute. (2021). Chile. www.tni.org/en/article/chile-the-battle-for-a-transformative-new-constitution.

Tocqueville, A. D. (1945). *Democracy in America*, New York: Vintage.

Treisman, D. (2007). *The Architecture of Government*, New York: Cambridge University Press.

Trindade, A. A. C. (2006). El Derecho Internacional de Los Derechos Humanos en el Siglo XXI. Santiago: Editorial Jurídica de Chile.

Tully, J. (2008). The Kantian Idea of Europe. In Tully, J. (ed.) *Imperialism and Civic Freedom*. Cambridge: Cambridge University Press, 15–42.

UN High Level Panel (2004). A More Secure World. *U.N. Doc A/59/565.*

Usman, A. & Falola, T. (eds.) (2019). *The Yoruba from Prehistory to the Present*, Cambridge: Cambridge University Press.

Van Kersbergen, K. & Verbeek, B. (1994). The Politics of Subsidiarity in the European Union. *Journal of Common Market Studies*, 32, 215–236.

(2007). The Politics of International Norms. *European Journal of International Relations*, 13, 217–238.

Van Til, K. (2008). Subsidiarity and Sphere Sovereignty – A Match Made In . . . ? *Theological Studies*, 69, 610–636.

Varden, H. (2017). Kant and Women. *Pacific Philosophical Quarterly*, 98, 653–694.

Viehoff, D. (2011). Procedure and Outcome in the Justification of Authority. *Journal of Political Philosophy*, 19, 248–259.

Von Nell-Breuning, O. (1962). Subsidiaritätsprinzip. In *Staatslexicon*. Freiburg: Herder, 826–833.

(1986). The Drafting of Quadragesimo Anno. In Curran, C. & McCormick, R. (eds.) *Official Catholic Social Teaching*. New York: Paulist Press, 60–68.

Von Staden, A. (2012). Democratic Legitimacy of Review Beyond the State. *International Journal of Constitutional Law*, 10, 1023–1049.

(2016a). Subsidiarity in Regional Integration Regimes in Latin America and Africa. *Law and Contemporary Problems*, 79, 27–52.

(2016b). Subsidiarity, Exhaustion of Domestic Remedies, and the Margin of Appreciation in the Human Rights Jurisprudence of African Sub-Regional Courts. *The International Journal of Human Rights*, 20, 1113–1131.

Waldron, J. (1987). Theoretical Foundations of Liberalism. *Philosophical Quarterly*, 37, 127–50.

(2013). Separation of Powers in Thought and Practice? *Boston College Law Review*, 54, 433–468.

Walker, A. & Wong, C. (eds.) (2005). *East Asian Welfare Regimes in Transition*, Briston: Policy Press.

Walther, R. (2022). *Subsidiarity: The ECHR between Law and Politics* (PhD Dissertation), University of Zürich.

(2025). *Subsidiarity, Legitimacy, and the European Court of Human Rights*, Oxford: Oxford University Press.

Wamala, E. Government by Consensus: An Analysis of a Traditional Form of Democracy. In Wiredu (ed.) *A Companion to African Philosophy*. Oxford: Blackwell, 435–442.

Wamba-Dia-Wamba, E. (1992). Beyond Elite Politics of Democracy in Africa. *Quest*, 28–43, 6.

Weale, A. (2020). *Modern Social Contract Theory*, Oxford: Oxford University Press.

Weber, M. (1972). Politics as a Vocation. In Gerth, H. & Mills, C. (eds.) *Max Weber*. New York: Oxford University Press, 77–128.

Wehr, H. & Cowan, J. (2020). *Dictionary of Modern Written Arabic (Fourth Edition)*, Hawthorne, CA: BN.

Weiler, J. H. H. (1991). The Transformation of Europe. *Yale Law Review*, 100, 1–81.

Weinberger, L. (2014). The Relationship between Sphere Sovereignty and Subsidiarity. In Zimmermann, A. & Evans, M. (eds.) *Global Perspectives on Subsidiarity*, Dordrecht: Springer, 49–63.

Weingast, B. (2014). Second Generation Fiscal Federalism. *World Development*, 53, 14–25.

Weinstock, D. (2014). Cities and Federalism. In Fleming, J. & Levy, J. (eds.) *Federalism and Subsidiarity*. New York: NYU Press, 259–290.

Whelan, F. G. (1983). Prologue. In Pennock, R. & Chapman, J. W. (eds.) *Liberal Democracy*. New York: Nomos, 13–47.

Williams, H. (1983). *Kant's Political Philosophy*, New York: St. Martin's Press.

(2012). *Kant and the End of War*, London: Palgrave.

(2014). Colonialism in Kant's Political Philosophy. *Diametros*, 39, 154–181.

Williams, M. (ed.) (2020). *Deparochializing Political Theory*, Cambridge: Cambridge University Press.

Wolff, C. (1736(1996)). Vernünfftige Gedancken Von Dem Gesellschaftlichen Leben Der Menschen und Insonderheit Dem Gemeinen Wesen. In École, J. (ed.) *Christian Wolff*. Hildesheim: G. Olms.

(1754). *Grundsätze Des Natur- und Völckerrechts*, Halle: Renger.

1728 (1966). Methodi Philosophicae Eaedem Sunt Regulae, Quae Methodi Mathematicae. In Gawlick, G. & Kreimendahl, L. (eds.) *Discursus Praeliminaris de Philosophia in Genere*. Stuttgart: Frommann.

Wood, A. T. (1995). *Limits to Autocracy*, Honolulu, HI: University of Hawaii Press.

Wood, A. (1999). *Kant's Ethical Thought*, New York: Cambridge University Press.

(2008). *Kantian Ethics*, Cambridge: Cambridge University Press.

Yoo, J. (2009). Hausa City States (Ca. 1000–1815). *BlackPast.org*.

Young, I. M. (2000). Hybrid Democracy. In Ivison, D., Patton, P., & Sanders, W. (eds.) *Political Theory and the Rights of Indigenous Peoples*. Cambridge: Cambridge University Press, 236–258.

Young, M. (ed.) (2012). *Regime Interaction in International Law*, Cambridge: Cambridge University Press.

Yourow, H. (1996). *The Margin of Appreciation Doctrine in the Dynamics of European Human Rights Jurisprudence*, Leiden: Brill.

Zhao, D. (2015). *The Confucian-Legalist State*, Oxford: Oxford University Press.

Zimmermann, A. & Evans, M. (eds.) (2014). *Global Perspectives on Subsidiarity*, Dordrecht: Springer.

Zürn, M. (2018). *A Theory of Global Governance*, Oxford: Oxford University Press.

Zysow, A. (2012). Zakat. In Bearman, P., Bosworth, C. E., van Donzel, E., & Heinrichset W. P. (eds.) *Encyclopaedia of Islam*. Leiden: Brill Reference, XI:406b.

Acknowledgements

This Element has benefited greatly from presentations and discussions over the last ten years, including at the 2015 AseanSIL Conference and the German-Southeast Asian Center at Thammasat University, Bangkok; in 2017 at a Conference on General Principles, Paris; the 2022 MANCEPT workshop 'After Subsidiarity?', a webinar on international legal theory, a seminar at the University of Richmond, and at EURAC, Bolzano. Thanks to RIPPLE at KU Leuven and Alejandra Mancilla and her ERC project Dynamic Territory, for a workshop 2022 on this manuscript. Special thanks to Francesco Palermo and colleagues at EURAC, Bolzano; Alejandro Chehtman at the University Torcuato Di Tella; and Paula Almeida at the FGV Centre for Global Law for research stays in 2022 and 2023. Wissenschaftskolleg zu Berlin provided an exceptionally supportive environment to complete the manuscript 2023–24.

I am grateful for detailed references and comments from many, my apologies for any names lost from memory and notes. They include two anonymous reviewers, Iveren Abiem, Oddný Mjöll Arnardóttir, Joel Blecher, François Boucher, Evan Criddle, Helder De Schutter, Paulina Espejo, Dorothea Gaedeke, Stian Øby Johansen, Jens Van 't Klooster, David Lefkowitz, Reidar Maliks, Alejandra Mancilla, Johan Olsthoorn, Carmen Pavel, Konstantinos Alexandris Polomarkakis, Emilia Powell, Steven Ratner, Michael Reiertsen, Nicole Roughan, Colin Rowe, Matt Saul, Jasmine Sommardal, Yanfei Sun, Oisin Suttle, Geir Ulfstein, Antonia Waltermann, Reto Walther, Pauline Westerman, Sun Xiangchen, and Dingxin Zhao. Responsibility for all mistakes remains mine.

Research for this Element was partly supported by the Research Council of Norway through its Centres of Excellence Funding Scheme, project number 223274 – PluriCourts: The Legitimacy of the International Judiciary based at the Faculty of Law, University of Oslo; and from Wissenschaftskolleg zu Berlin.

Cambridge Elements

Philosophy of Law

About the Series

This series provides an accessible overview of the philosophy of law, drawing on its varied intellectual traditions in order to showcase the interdisciplinary dimensions of jurisprudential enquiry, review the state of the art in the field, and suggest fresh research agendas for the future. Focussing on issues rather than traditions or authors, each contribution seeks to deepen our understanding of the foundations of the law, ultimately with a view to offering practical insights into some of the major challenges of our age.

Cambridge Elements

Philosophy of Law

Elements in the Series

The Materiality of the Legal Order
Marco Goldoni

Sociological Approaches to Theories of Law
Brian Z. Tamanaha

Revisiting the Rule of Law
Kristen Rundle

The Place of Coercion in Law
Triantafyllos Gkouvas

The Differentiation and Autonomy of Law
Emilios Christodoulidis

The Moral Prerequisites of the Criminal Law: Legal Moralism and the Problem of Mala Prohibita
Ambrose Y. K. Lee and Alexander F. Sarch

Legal Personhood
Visa A. J. Kurki

The Philosophy of Legal Proof
Lewis Ross

The Normativity of Law
Michael Giudice

Legal Rights and Moral Rights
Matthew H. Kramer

Dignity and Rights
Ariel Zylberman

Subsidiarity
Andreas Follesdal

A full series listing is available at: www.cambridge.org/EPHL

For EU product safety concerns, contact us at Calle de José Abascal, 56–1°, 28003 Madrid, Spain or eugpsr@cambridge.org.

www.ingramcontent.com/pod-product-compliance
Ingram Content Group UK Ltd.
Pitfield, Milton Keynes, MK11 3LW, UK
UKHW022147080726
473066UK00010B/812

* 9 7 8 1 1 0 8 9 9 5 2 3 8 *